Water

Other Books of Related Interest:

At Issue Series
Food Safety
Should There Be an International Climate Treaty?
Should the U.S. Reduce Its Consumption?
Wave and Tidal Power

Global Viewpoints Series
Air Pollution
Garbage and Recycling

Introducing Issues with Opposing Viewpoints Series
Energy Alternatives
Oceans

Issues That Concern You Series
Climate Change
Going Green

Opposing Viewpoints Series
Coal
Epidemics
Pollution

GLOBALVIEWPOINTS

Water

Noah Berlatsky, Book Editor

GREENHAVEN PRESS
A part of Gale, Cengage Learning

GALE
CENGAGE Learning

Detroit • New York • San Francisco • New Haven, Conn • Waterville, Maine • London

Elizabeth Des Chenes, *Managing Editor*

© 2012 Greenhaven Press, a part of Gale, Cengage Learning

Gale and Greenhaven Press are registered trademarks used herein under license.

For more information, contact:
Greenhaven Press
27500 Drake Rd.
Farmington Hills, MI 48331-3535
Or you can visit our Internet site at gale.cengage.com

ALL RIGHTS RESERVED.
No part of this work covered by the copyright herein may be reproduced, transmitted, stored, or used in any form or by any means graphic, electronic, or mechanical, including but not limited to photocopying, recording, scanning, digitizing, taping, Web distribution, information networks, or information storage and retrieval systems, except as permitted under Section 107 or 108 of the 1976 United States Copyright Act, without the prior written permission of the publisher.

For product information and technology assistance, contact us at

Gale Customer Support, 1-800-877-4253
For permission to use material from this text or product, submit all requests online at www.cengage.com/permissions

Further permissions questions can be emailed to permissionrequest@cengage.com

Articles in Greenhaven Press anthologies are often edited for length to meet page requirements. In addition, original titles of these works are changed to clearly present the main thesis and to explicitly indicate the author's opinion. Every effort is made to ensure that Greenhaven Press accurately reflects the original intent of the authors. Every effort has been made to trace the owners of copyrighted material.

Cover image copyright © Karen Kasmauski/Terra/Corbis.

LIBRARY OF CONGRESS CATALOGING-IN-PUBLICATION DATA

Water / Noah Berlatsky, book editor.
    p. cm. -- (Global viewpoints)
    Includes bibliographical references and index.
    ISBN 978-0-7377-5666-1 (hardcover : alk. paper) -- ISBN 978-0-7377-5667-8 (pbk. : alk. paper)
    1. Water--Environmental aspects. 2. Water supply. 3. Water use. I. Berlatsky, Noah.
    GB662.3.W372 2011
    363.6'1--dc23
                                                                    2011018411

Printed in the USA
2 3 4 5 6   30 29 28 27 26

Contents

Foreword   11

Introduction   14

Chapter 1: The Oceans

1. **Ireland** Will Be Hurt by Sea-Level Rise Due to Global Warming   20
   Kieran R. Hickey

   As an island nation, Ireland is especially vulnerable to the flooding and coastal erosion that will result as global warming causes sea levels to rise. Managing sea-level rise will cost Ireland billions of euros.

2. **Australian** Sea-Level Rise Due to Global Warming Has Been Exaggerated   27
   Drew Warne-Smith and James Madden

   Sea levels in Australia are rising less than two millimeters a year, which is in line with historical trends. Recent aggressive government actions, based on global warming fears, appear to be unjustified.

3. Acidification Threatens the World's Oceans   34
   Severin Carrell

   Carbon emissions are increasing the acidity of the oceans. The acidity threatens marine life such as corals and plankton, and it may reduce fishing catches and lead to extinctions of some species.

4. The Seriousness of Ocean Acidification Is Overstated   39
   Matt Ridley

   The danger of ocean acidification is exaggerated. Reported changes in acidity are within natural variation. Moreover, increased levels of carbon dioxide in the ocean may actually help coral and other marine life.

5. The Pacific Ocean's Garbage Patch Should Be Cleaned Up   43
   Paul Van Slambrouck

Sailor and activist Mary Crowley is organizing fishermen to help clean up a giant shoal of plastic debris in the northern Pacific Ocean. They hope to recycle the plastic and reduce ocean pollution.

6. Cleaning Up the Plastic in the Oceans 49
   Will Accomplish Little
   Richard Grant

   Plastic is so prevalent in the oceans that cleaning up the Great Pacific Garbage Patch is not an effective solution. Instead, people need to change the way they use plastics.

Periodical and Internet Sources Bibliography 61

Chapter 2: Managing Water Scarcity

1. Climate Shifts and Human Action Have Caused 63
   Irreversible Desertification in the **Sahel**
   Alex Shoumatoff

   The Sahel region in Africa is being irreversibly turned into desert; global warming and overpopulation resulting in rapid clearing of land are probably responsible.

2. Human Action Is Reversing Desertification 71
   in the **Sahel**
   Mae-Wan Ho and Lim Li Ching

   The desertification of the Sahel was due to normal climate variation. Planting initiatives have helped to mitigate the process, and currently the Sahel is becoming green again.

3. **China**'s Water Crisis May Be Helped 80
   by Trading Water Rights
   Zhou Jigang, Peng Guangcan, and Ceng Zhen

   China has been suffering from a severe water shortage. This has resulted in conflicts over access to water between different regions and interests. China is having some success with solving these problems by setting up a market-based system for trading water rights.

4. **Chile**'s System of Trading Water Rights 88
   Has Hurt Citizens and the Environment
   Benjamin Witte

Chile has long had a privatized water market in which water rights can be bought and sold. Critics argue that this system privileges the powerful at the expense of ordinary people. They are attempting to nationalize Chile's water.

5. **Israel** Steals **Palestinian** Water, Resulting in a Water Crisis   94
   Sawsan Ramahi
   Israel has control of most of the water resources of the Palestinian territory. It diverts these resources for its own use, creating painful water shortages in the territories.

6. The **Middle East** Water Crisis Is the Result of the Failures of Many Regional Governments   106
   Gidon Bromberg
   The water shortage in the Middle East is a region-wide problem that may result in the drying up of the Jordan River. The water crisis is the result of poor management by and conflict between countries including Jordan, Syria, and Israel.

7. **Nile River** Countries Struggle over Water Rights   113
   Joshua Kyalimpa
   Lake Victoria, which feeds the Nile, is shrinking. Egypt, Sudan, Uganda, and other countries that use the Nile are trying to reach an agreement to preserve its water. If they fail, conservation and developmental goals may be unreachable.

Periodical and Internet Sources Bibliography   119

Chapter 3: Access to Safe Water

1. **China**'s Poor Environmental Record Has Poisoned Water Supplies   121
   Andreas Lorenz
   A chemical plant catastrophe on the Songhua River has poisoned the water. The tragedy shows the downside of China's economic expansion and the inadequate response of its leaders.

2. **Haiti**'s Cholera Outbreak Highlights Clean Water Crisis   128
   Ansel Herz

Months after a devastating earthquake in Haiti there remains only limited access to clean, uncontaminated water. This shortage has resulted in a deadly cholera outbreak.

3. **Bangladesh** Is Trying to Establish Arsenic-Free Wells 135
   IRIN News

   Many wells in Bangladesh are contaminated with arsenic, which can cause illness and, after prolonged exposure, death. Health organizations and the government are attempting to address the problem.

4. **India** Must Focus on Clean Water for Children 140
   Craig Kielburger and Marc Kielburger

   Many Indian children lack access to clean water. Because children do not vote and lack political power, this issue has received less attention from India's government than it should.

5. Desalination Can Help Address the World's Clean Water Shortage 145
   The Economist

   Desalination, or removing salt from seawater, is one way to help address the worldwide need for clean water. New technology has made the process more affordable and less environmentally damaging.

Periodical and Internet Sources Bibliography 156

Chapter 4: Hydropower

1. In **Uganda**, Hydroelectric Dams Provide Needed Electricity 158
   Christopher M. Walsh and Steven Shalita

   Hydropower from dams can significantly increase access to electricity for Ugandans and other Africans. Environmental concerns should be taken seriously, but must be balanced with the need for electricity.

2. In **Brazil**, Hydroelectric Dams Threaten Communities and the Environment 164
   Joshua Partlow

Brazil is planning to build dams on the Madeira River to generate electricity. Critics say the dam will damage a rich ecological area and force the relocation of indigenous peoples.

3. Wave Power May Become an Important Source of Green Energy in **Europe** 170
Mark Scott

Many projects are moving forward to harness marine power in different parts of Europe. There is hope that wave power can generate significant energy with few environmental effects.

4. In **Portugal**, Wave Power Projects Have Failed 176
Alan Copps

An Edinburgh-based company working on a wave energy project in Portugal has faced setbacks. These include equipment failure and financial difficulties. The problems may derail further wave energy programs by the company.

5. In **France**, Tidal Power Has Been Successful 180
Robert Williams

France since the 1960s has had a functional and effective tidal power station. As fossil fuels become more expensive, France's station may become a model for growth in tidal power.

6. Tidal Power Is Not Economically or Environmentally Feasible in **Britain**'s Severn Estuary 186
HM Government, Department of Energy and Climate Change

A plan to harness the tidal power of the Severn estuary is not feasible. Building the necessary tidal barrages would be much more expensive and would cause more environmental damage than other clean-energy options.

Periodical and Internet Sources Bibliography	194
For Further Discussion	195
Organizations to Contact	197
Bibliography of Books	202
Index	205

Foreword

> "The problems of all of humanity can
> only be solved by all of humanity."
> —Swiss author Friedrich Dürrenmatt

Global interdependence has become an undeniable reality. Mass media and technology have increased worldwide access to information and created a society of global citizens. Understanding and navigating this global community is a challenge, requiring a high degree of information literacy and a new level of learning sophistication.

Building on the success of its flagship series, Opposing Viewpoints, Greenhaven Press has created the Global Viewpoints series to examine a broad range of current, often controversial topics of worldwide importance from a variety of international perspectives. Providing students and other readers with the information they need to explore global connections and think critically about worldwide implications, each Global Viewpoints volume offers a panoramic view of a topic of widespread significance.

Drugs, famine, immigration—a broad, international treatment is essential to do justice to social, environmental, health, and political issues such as these. Junior high, high school, and early college students, as well as general readers, can all use Global Viewpoints anthologies to discern the complexities relating to each issue. Readers will be able to examine unique national perspectives while, at the same time, appreciating the interconnectedness that global priorities bring to all nations and cultures.

Material in each volume is selected from a diverse range of sources, including journals, magazines, newspapers, nonfiction books, speeches, government documents, pamphlets, organization newsletters, and position papers. Global Viewpoints is truly global, with material drawn primarily from international sources available in English and secondarily from US sources with extensive international coverage.

Features of each volume in the Global Viewpoints series include:

- An **annotated table of contents** that provides a brief summary of each essay in the volume, including the name of the country or area covered in the essay.

- An **introduction** specific to the volume topic.

- A **world map** to help readers locate the countries or areas covered in the essays.

- For each viewpoint, an **introduction** that contains notes about the author and source of the viewpoint explains why material from the specific country is being presented, summarizes the main points of the viewpoint, and offers three **guided reading questions** to aid in understanding and comprehension.

- **For further discussion** questions that promote critical thinking by asking the reader to compare and contrast aspects of the viewpoints or draw conclusions about perspectives and arguments.

- A worldwide list of **organizations to contact** for readers seeking additional information.

- A **periodical bibliography** for each chapter and a **bibliography of books** on the volume topic to aid in further research.

- A comprehensive **subject index** to offer access to people, places, events, and subjects cited in the text, with the countries covered in the viewpoints highlighted.

Foreword

Global Viewpoints is designed for a broad spectrum of readers who want to learn more about current events, history, political science, government, international relations, economics, environmental science, world cultures, and sociology—students doing research for class assignments or debates, teachers and faculty seeking to supplement course materials, and others wanting to understand current issues better. By presenting how people in various countries perceive the root causes, current consequences, and proposed solutions to worldwide challenges, Global Viewpoints volumes offer readers opportunities to enhance their global awareness and their knowledge of cultures worldwide.

Introduction

> *"Humans have tried to control the waters with levees and dams, essentially rerouting Mother Nature using a complex network of barriers. But the most massive engineering projects can often lead to even more complex problems, experts say—especially if planners fail to prepare for the worst."*
>
> —Jeremy Hsu,
> "Man vs. Nature:
> Why Floods Still Win,"
> LiveScience, August 25, 2010

Human beings are profoundly affected by floods. Many human civilizations began around rivers like the Nile and the Indus, where seasonal floods deposited mud and rich soil on the banks, creating good conditions for agriculture. In modern times, on the other hand, floods have often caused catastrophic destruction. In 2010, for example, summer floods in Pakistan caused $9.5 billion dollars in damage. According to an October 13, 2010, report by Sahar Ahmed for Reuters, "The floods, which began in late July, left more than 10 million people homeless and affected 20 million, and devastated an economy that was already fragile before one of the country's worst natural disasters." The floods killed more than fifteen hundred people.

Since flooding can be so devastating, many experts and commentators have tried to understand how, and whether, human beings are affecting the likelihood or intensity of floods. Recent debates have focused especially on the links between global warming and flooding. For example, Julian Hunt, a professor at Delft University of Technology, argued in an

August 27, 2010, article for the *Sydney Morning Herald* that the 2010 Pakistan floods may have been tied to climate change. The warming temperature, he said, might have created a "less stable atmosphere" which in turn "caused deeper convection and intense rainfall." He argued that such changes could be responsible for the intense rainfall in Pakistan and other parts of South Asia. Similarly, Hurricane Katrina, which catastrophically flooded New Orleans, Louisiana, in 2005, has been blamed on changing climate. As Ross Gelbspan wrote in the August 30, 2005, *Boston Globe*, "The hurricane that struck Louisiana yesterday was nicknamed Katrina by the National Weather Service. Its real name is global warming."

However, some scientists have argued that global warming is not likely to contribute significantly to flooding. A study by Thomas R. Knutson et al. in *Nature Geoscience* attempted to determine how warming would affect the large storms that often trigger floods. The study estimated that "greenhouse warming will cause the globally averaged intensity of tropical cyclones to shift towards stronger storms, with intensity increases of 2–11% by 2100. Existing modelling studies also consistently project decreases in the globally averaged frequency of tropical cyclones, by 6–34%." In other words, global warming is actually likely to *decrease* the number of intense storms. At the same time, the storms that remain are likely to be slightly stronger in intensity. Overall, these changes seem unlikely to lead to an increase in overall worldwide flooding.

There has also been a scientific debate over whether deforestation—or the large-scale cutting down of trees—contributes to flooding. Corey J.A. Bradshaw et al., in a November 2007 article in *Global Change Biology*, analyzed ten years of flood data to look for links between forestation and flooding. They determined that "as little as 10% loss in natural forest cover can increase flood frequency from 4 to 28%," according to a summary on the Charles Darwin University website. The same summary quoted Bradshaw as saying, "Our empirical results indicate that halting deforestation or reducing the rate of natural forest loss should be beneficial in alleviating the incidence and severity of floods that ultimately cause undesirable disruption and damage to human life and property."

A 2005 report by the Food and Agriculture Organization of the United Nations and the Center for International Forestry Research, however, found no link between deforestation and flooding. The report argued that "contrary to popular belief, forests have only a limited influence on major downstream flooding, especially large-scale events." The report concluded that "large-scale reforestation programmes, the adoption of soil and water conservation technologies in agriculture, logging bans and the resettlement of upland people to lowland areas will *not* significantly reduce the incidence or severity of catastrophic floods."

One way in which humans have successfully mitigated flooding is through building dams. The Netherlands, a country largely below sea level, has been particularly aggressive in dam building. Following a flood that killed two thousand people in 1953, the Dutch built an extensive system of advanced storm surge barriers. They also constructed "a series of dams and levees between water and city—rather than just one layer," according to an August 1, 2006, report by the American Institute of Physics' *Discoveries and Breakthroughs Inside Science* broadcasting series.

Despite Dutch success, not everyone has been convinced that dams are the best way to control flooding. Willem Vervoort, a professor of hydrology at the University of Sydney in Australia, argued that dams were not the best flood-control measure in a January 12, 2011, article in the *Sydney Morning Herald*. According to Vervoort, dams provide a false sense of security; people believe they are 100 percent safe, even though there is always some chance of flooding. Vervoort also pointed out that dams damage the environment, changing water flow and altering ecosystems. Instead of building dams, he recommended moving homes in the way of floods, improving flood forecasting, and helping people to be prepared for flooding. "Learning to live with floods rather than preparing to fight floods will lead to a more resilient and prosperous future and allow us to take full advantage of our variable climate," Vervoort concluded.

Global Viewpoints: Water focuses on other controversies surrounding the interaction of water and people in chapters titled "The Oceans," "Managing Water Scarcity," "Access to Safe Water," and "Hydropower." Water is vital to human life and to the planet; its regulation, distribution, and safety continue to be the occasion for conflict, debate, and study.

Water

The Oceans

VIEWPOINT 1

Ireland Will Be Hurt by Sea-Level Rise Due to Global Warming

Kieran R. Hickey

Kieran R. Hickey is a professor in the Department of Geography at the National University of Ireland in Galway and the author of Five Minutes to Midnight? Ireland and Climate Change. *In the following viewpoint, he argues that sea-level rise associated with global warming poses a serious threat to Ireland. He says that global warming will cause expansion of water and possible melting of polar ice caps. As a result, seas will rise, and Ireland, which is an island nation, will face devastating floods and dangerous coastal erosion. Hickey concludes that the government will need to spend billions of euros to protect Ireland from these threats.*

As you read, consider the following questions:

1. According to Hickey, why was sea level much lower at the end of the last ice age thirteen thousand years ago?
2. What is the problem with water level data from the tide gauges in Ireland, according to Hickey?
3. What kinds of coastlines in Ireland does Hickey say are *not* under threat?

Kieran R. Hickey, "Sea-Level Rise . . . Will Cost Ireland Billions," thelocalplanet.ie, October 21, 2005. www.thelocalplanet.ie. Copyright © 2005 by Kieran R. Hickey. All rights reserved. Reproduced by permission.

The Oceans

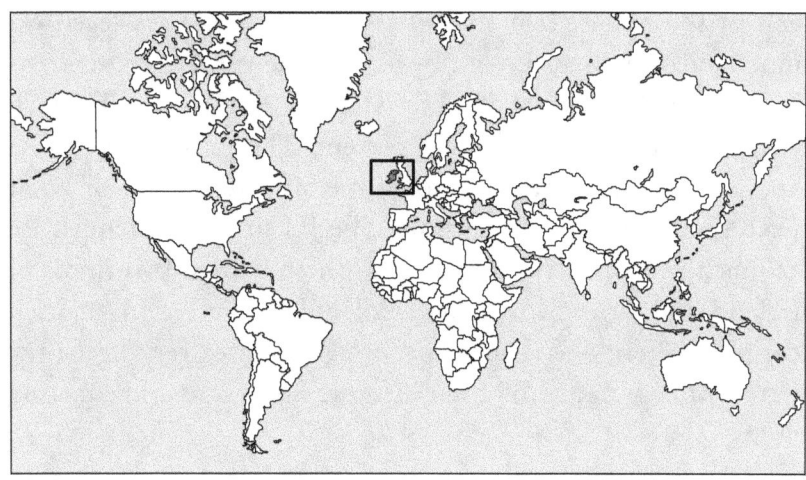

One of the key aspects of the current concern over global warming is the predictions for sea-level rise and the likely impact of this. This aspect of the whole global warming story is poorly understood by most and yet it will have the greatest impact on Ireland, of that there is no doubt. Even though the climate of Ireland will get warmer with more seasonality of rainfall which could lead to increased flooding in winter and water shortages in summer especially in the eastern half of Ireland. This will not have a big impact on the country with the exception of agriculture where some adjustments may have to be made. At the moment however the lengthening of the growing season for grass by a number of weeks over the last 30 years or so is of benefit to farmers in Ireland.

In my opinion the real threat to Ireland comes from ongoing and enhanced sea-level rise and associated with this increased coastal and estuarine flooding, first we need to understand what sea-level change is about, what is the current evidence for it and what are the drivers behind it and why it is such a threat.

Sea-level change is a normal part of the response of the oceans and ice areas to climate change. If we go back to the end of the last ice age around 13,000 years ago sea level was much lower than at present by as much as 80–100 m; this was because huge volumes of freshwater were locked up in much larger ice sheets than exist at present. The current ice sheets and ice caps around the globe are only remnants of what would have existed at this time. The last ice age extended ice as much as 1km deep over most of the northern two-thirds of Ireland and is known as the Midlandian Ice Age in an Irish context. There was also a localised ice cap over the Cork-Kerry Mts. because of their height. So this is our starting point.

> *The real threat to Ireland comes from ongoing and enhanced sea-level rise and associated with this increased coastal and estuarine flooding.*

As the climate warmed up at the end of the last ice age these huge volumes of ice began to melt and retreat polarward or altitudinally. This released huge volumes of water into the oceans which began to rise and this rise has been occurring since then with some variations due to periods such as the Little Ice Age AD1450–1850 when there is some evidence to suggest a small growth in ice sheets and glaciers. Since then however there has been a consistent rise in sea level on a global basis at most sites so much so that from 1900 to 2000 the global average was between 10 and 15cm and in many cases the rate of the rise is accelerating. The exceptions to this are areas which were under heavy ice sheets including the northern half of Ireland which because of the weight of the ice depressed the earth's crust, which is still rebounding since the ice melted. This complicates the story a little bit but we can mostly ignore this.

Most of the current sea-level rise which has been going on since the mid-1800s is due to the thermal expansion of water as it heats up, just in the same way as you would boil a kettle. However, this masks the real concern which is that there is going to be a substantial melting of the world's ice areas including many glaciers in places such as the Alps, Andes and other great mountain ranges. There is no doubt that most of the world's mountain glaciers are melting, some have melted entirely even though they were photographed as little as 30 years ago. But even if they all melted they would add very little to global sea-level rise. Of much more critical concern is that the world's major ice caps would melt in particular in Greenland and Antarctica. If the entire Greenland Ice Sheet was to melt the release of water would raise global sea level by around 6 metres. If even a relatively small part of the Antarctic melted it could raise global sea level by 10s of metres. The world would be a very different place if any of these events were to happen.

Current measures of sea-level change in Ireland are based on water level data from a number of tide gauges throughout the island of Ireland. Unfortunately nearly all these records do not go back into the 1800s to give us a good picture of the long-term trend.

But it is clear that at the moment in the northern half of Ireland sea-level rise and land-level rise are roughly about even so there is no net change, however in the southern half of Ireland as well as sea-level rise being recorded there is also land-level fall so the effect of sea-level rise is being enhanced. The predictions and the evidence suggest that as sea-level rise accelerates then even in the northern half of Ireland the sea-level rise will be faster than the land-level rise and the rate of sea-level rise in the southern half of Ireland will be far greater. Currently, the predictions for global sea-level rise assuming no catastrophic ice sheet melt is from 15cm to 90cm by 2100 far in excess of the rate for the 20th century. This is the background to the threat, let's now look at the threat in Ireland's context.

Water

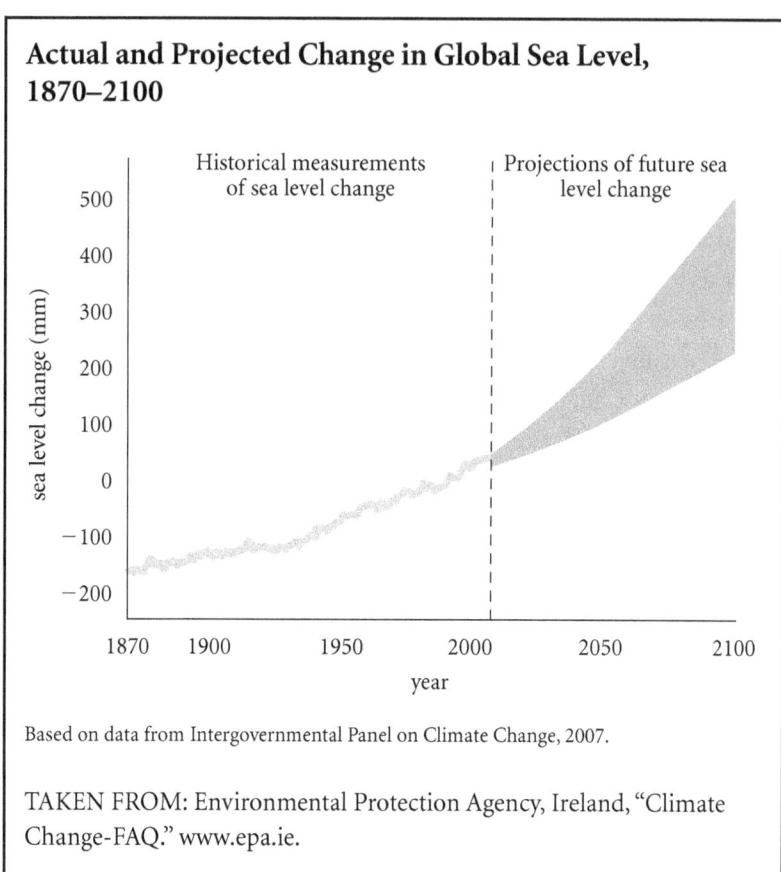

Actual and Projected Change in Global Sea Level, 1870–2100

Based on data from Intergovernmental Panel on Climate Change, 2007.

TAKEN FROM: Environmental Protection Agency, Ireland, "Climate Change-FAQ." www.epa.ie.

> *Of much more critical concern is that the world's major ice caps would melt in particular in Greenland and Antarctica.*

Ireland is an island nation, all our major urban areas are either coastal or estuarine including Belfast, Dublin, Waterford, Cork, Limerick, Galway and Derry to name the major ones. In 2002 Dublin experienced significant coastal flooding so much so that the current estimate for urgent flood barriers for the city to prevent a recurrence is 100 million euro out of a current government budget of around 25 million euro for this type of work for the whole country. Cork and Waterford have experienced major flooding in 2004, and all the other coastal cities and towns have all records of coastal or estuarine flooding, so they are already vulnerable to sea-level rise not to mention what is likely to happen in the future. Although all these events are associated with big storms what is happening is that on top of the normal tidal cycle with high and low tides a storm effectively pushes a block of water in front of it and this tops up the usual water level. These storms stop the removal of water from rivers as happened in 2004 when flooding became widespread in the Suir Valley as far inland as Clonmel. As sea-level rise continues the potential for big storms to raise water levels higher and higher well beyond existing record levels increases significantly so it's not a question of if but when. This will increase the areas flooded and the severity of flooding. The impact of Hurricane Katrina on New Orleans should be a clear example to everyone of the potential destruction that could occur.

The rest of the coastlines of Ireland are also under threat with the exception of rock cliff coastlines which are very resilient to attack. For low coastlines made up of sand, mud and loose rock, particularly the east and south coasts but also in many parts of the west and north coastlines. As sea-level rise occurs high tides will penetrate further inland and lead to increased coastal erosion especially if storm intensity changes. Currently average erosion rates of between 1 and 2m are occurring in parts of the east coast of Ireland, this figure could rise dramatically. Not only will this reduce the size of our beaches and sand dunes it will also cause the loss of agricultural land, whole farms have disappeared into the sea since they were first recorded in the 1st edition of the Ordnance Survey in the 1840s. There is also a great potential for damage to coastal aquifers through salinization and once they become salty they are not suitable for use by humans and animals and it is almost impossible to remove the salt. This could have a big impact on coastal rural areas which rely on local water schemes.

From a government perspective the treatment of our coastlines has been very poor, currently the county councils are responsible for coastal protection on a piecemeal basis and with limited budgets to tackle the problem. The cost of coastal protection is very high involving millions of euro per km protected for rural coastlines whereas high-value urban coastal areas will have to be protected even though the cost per km is much higher. We cannot afford to protect all the coastline of Ireland because of its length and complexity. Sadly, although a very extensive integrated national coastal zone management strategy was developed by consultants Brady Shipman Martin involving a huge effort by all the stakeholders from government departments right down to local groups and which would have covered the whole country and would be completely integrated, this was shelved by the then government, so no change has taken place. Even a basic idea of not allowing any new development where ground floor entry level is below 5m ... has not been implemented even though it represents a sensible response to the potential threat.

This article presents a very grim picture of sea-level rise and its likely impact on Ireland, but if we get away with no catastrophic ice melt from one of the world's major ice sheets over the next 100 years then we will have done well. With an integrated central government approach to the issue we should be able to manage the expected sea-level rise up to 2100, but it will cost us billions of euro in terms of defences and compensation. Tough political decisions will have to be made.

VIEWPOINT

Australian Sea-Level Rise Due to Global Warming Has Been Exaggerated

Drew Warne-Smith and James Madden

Drew Warne-Smith and James Madden are Australian journalists. In the following viewpoint, they report that sea-level rise in Australia has been much less than predicted according to tidal gauges and some experts. In fact, they say, sea-level change seems to be in line with historical averages. The decision of New South Wales to ban the development of coastal sites seems unnecessary and alarmist, the authors suggest. However, they also report that some climate change experts still believe Australia will experience rapid and potentially dangerous sea-level rise.

As you read, consider the following questions:

1. How much does Nathan Rees say sea level will rise by 2050? How long do the authors suggest it will take before sea levels reach this height?
2. Why does Bill Kininmonth not believe that there will be significant sea-level rise?
3. What factor does John Church say may have partially offset increases in sea levels?

Drew Warne-Smith and James Madden, "Science Is In on Climate Change Sea-Level Rise: 1.7 mm," *The Australian*, November 7, 2009. Copyright © 2009 by *The Australian*. All rights reserved. Reproduced by permission.

Water

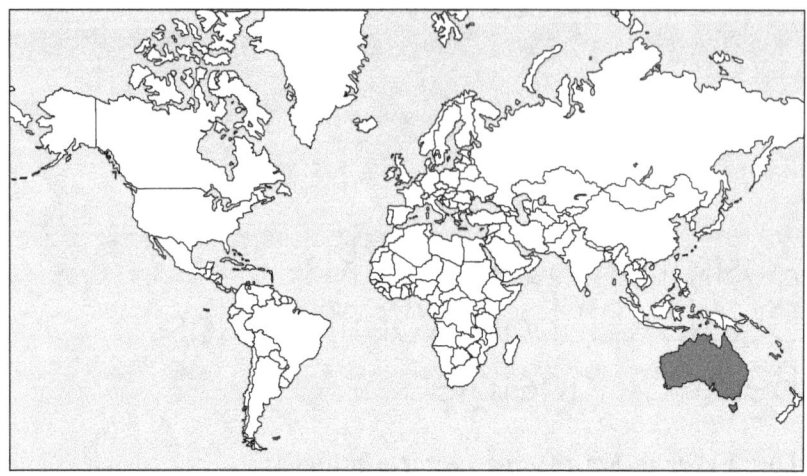

Sea levels on Australia's eastern seaboard are rising at less than a third of the rate that the NSW [New South Wales] government is predicting as it overhauls the state's planning laws and bans thousands of landowners from developing coastal sites.

A Small Rise

The [NSW premier Nathan] Rees government this week [November 2009] warned that coastal waters would rise 40cm [centimetres] on 1990 levels by 2050, with potentially disastrous effects.

Even yesterday Kevin Rudd [prime minister of Australia] warned in a speech to the Lowy Institute [for International Policy] that 700,000 homes and businesses, valued at up to $150 billion, were at risk from the surging tide.

However, if current sea-level rises continue, it would not be until about 2200—another 191 years—before the east coast experienced the kind of increases that have been flagged.

According to the most recent report by the Bureau of Meteorology's National Tidal Centre, issued in June, there has been an average yearly increase of 1.9mm [millimetres] in the combined net rate of relative sea level at Port Kembla, south of Sydney, since the station was installed in 1991.

This is consistent with historical analysis showing that, throughout the 20th century, there was a modest rise in global sea levels of about 20cm, or 1.7mm per year on average.

If current sea-level rises continue, it would not be until about 2200—another 191 years—before the east coast experienced the kind of increases that have been flagged.

By comparison, the NSW government's projections—based on global modelling by the Intergovernmental Panel on Climate Change [IPCC] as well as CSIRO [Commonwealth Scientific and Industrial Research Organisation, Australia's national science agency] regional analysis—equate to a future rise of about 6.6mm a year. Such a projection has caused widespread concern for landowners and developers, derision from "climate sceptics" within the scientific community and even some head-scratching from Wollongong locals such as Kevin Court, 80.

"I have swum at this beach every day for the past 50 years, and nothing much changes here," Mr Court said yesterday as he emerged from the surf at Wollongong's North Beach, just a short paddle from the Port Kembla gauging station.

"All this talk about rising sea levels—most of us old-timers haven't seen any change and we've been coming down here for decades.

"A few years ago part of the bank at the back of the beach was eroded. But you look at it now, and all the grass has grown back over it. The water hasn't washed back there for years.

"And that's nature. It's up and down, it comes and goes in cycles—nothing dramatic."

Nothing Unusual

The complex task of tracking sea levels is being performed by the Australian Baseline Sea Level Monitoring Project, which is co-ordinated by the National Tidal Centre.

The project operates 16 gauging stations around the country, with the eastern seaboard monitored by stations at Port Kembla, as well as Rosslyn Bay and Cape Ferguson, in Queensland.

Bob Carter, a geologist and environmental scientist with James Cook University in Queensland, said he was "baffled" as to why states and local councils would develop policy based primarily on global averages and not the records of local tidal gauges.

> "There have been lots of times in our history when sea levels rose as much or more than now," Professor Carter said. "There is nothing unusual in our current situation."

In the past year, the Port Kembla gauge has recorded a sea-level rise of just 0.1mm

"When you design a house in Sydney, do you entrust the architect and builder to do the heating and air-conditioning based on global average temperature? Of course not," Professor Carter said.

He added that even if seas were rising as much as 3.3mm a year—the CSIRO's current global estimate—they would remain within the bounds of natural and normal variation. "There have been lots of times in our history when sea levels rose as much or more than now," Professor Carter said. "There is nothing unusual in the current situation."

Meteorologist Bill [William] Kininmonth, former head of the National Climate Centre, is another to express concern about the way future sea-level rises have been modelled. Mr Kininmonth believes only a thin layer of the ocean is actually warming—about 200m [metres]—making it unlikely the oceans are expanding to any great degree.

He said there was little compelling evidence that the polar caps were melting and causing sea levels to rise.

Computer models also tended to underestimate the way evaporation regulated temperature, thereby exaggerating future temperature predictions, Mr Kininmonth added. "There's little reason to think the little bit of extra heat generated by greenhouse gases will make a dramatic difference," he said.

However, the consensus view of the scientific community remains that sea levels are rising at an accelerated rate because of human activity that has warmed Earth.

Experts Believe Sea Is Rising

The CSIRO's John Church, considered one of the world's leading authorities on sea-level rise, told the *Weekend Australian* yesterday he remained convinced waters along the eastern seaboard were rising in line with global averages. He noted that the BOM's [Bureau of Meteorology's] gauge results for Port Kembla as published here did not include the effect of barometric pressure, which, if included, would lift the sea-level increase to 3.1mm, not much less than agreed global estimates.

The Australian continent was also rising slightly—about 0.3–0.4mm a year around Sydney—which had partially offset increases in sea levels, he said. And an analysis of records from a gauge at Fort Denison in Sydney Harbour—not incorporated in the National Tidal Centre report—also revealed that, after 1950, periods of extreme sea-level rises occurred three times as frequently as in the first half of that century.

"There is a clear acceleration in the rate of sea-level rise," Dr Church said. "In the last 20 years, it's almost twice the global average for the 20th century."

Ice Sheet Melt Will Not Raise Sea Levels

Al Gore [in the film *An Inconvenient Truth*] raises the spectre of massive ice sheet destruction from Greenland and Antarctica to raise sea levels by 10–15 m [metres]. There is every reason to believe that the Greenland and Antarctic ice sheets are stable despite some peripheral melting at low elevations during the brief summer.

- The Greenland ice sheet has been preserved despite previous interglacials that were warmer than current temperatures. It has likely been in place for more than a million years.... Melting around the coastal margins and surging glaciers are not evidence of instability and there is no evidence of recent rapid sea-level rise.

- Arctic sea ice has a natural rhythm of expansion and contraction between winter and summer and year-to-year variations are small.... It would require a strong surge of relatively warm water into the Arctic basin to prevent the formation of sea ice in the long winter darkness.

- The Antarctic Circumpolar Current ... prevents the intrusion of warmer subtropical surface water to the Antarctic coastal margins. In addition, the wind stress causes upwelling of cold subsurface water on the poleward margin of the current.... There is no compelling evidence that the Antarctic ice sheet is other than in mass balance.

- Touted warming and ice shelf destruction are mainly confined to the Antarctic Peninsula that extends equatorward towards South America, a small fraction of the total ice mass.

William Kininmonth,
Unmasking: "An Inconvenient Truth,"
Center for Science and Public Policy, February 2007.

Dr Church said the NSW coast was likely to experience sea-level rises greater than global estimates due to changes in the wind stress patterns in the Pacific Ocean, which will strengthen the East Australian Current. And if polar ice caps were indeed melting at a significant rate—which is not yet established—Australia could witness even bigger swells still.

The CSIRO's John Church, considered one of the world's leading authorities on sea-level rise, . . . remained convinced waters along the eastern seaboard were rising in line with global averages.

Dr Church challenged Mr Kininmonth's assertion that only a thin surface layer of the ocean was warming, saying recent studies provided evidence of deep ocean warming although it couldn't be quantified as yet.

A spokesperson for the NSW Department of Environment, Climate Change and Water said NSW had selected the upper end of the IPCC modelling predictions because both emissions and measured global sea-level rise were now at or above the upper IPCC estimates.

VIEWPOINT 3

Acidification Threatens the World's Oceans

Severin Carrell

Severin Carrell is the Scotland correspondent for the Guardian. *In the following viewpoint, he reports on a new study that shows that carbon emissions are increasing the acidity of the oceans. Carrell says that acidity threatens marine life and that it may reduce fishing catches and lead to extinctions. He reports that scientists say the only way to combat ocean acidification is to reduce carbon emissions immediately.*

As you read, consider the following questions:
1. What key parts of the marine environment does the acidification report say will be severely affected by 2050?
2. How will ocean acidification affect whales and dolphins, according to Carrell?
3. Why does Brian Baird believe the acidification study will help to counter climate change skeptics?

The world's oceans are becoming acidic at a faster rate than at any time in the last 55m[illion] years, threatening disaster for marine life and food supplies across the globe, delegates at the UN [United Nations] climate conference in Copenhagen have been warned.

Severin Carrell, "Ocean Acidification Rates Pose Disaster for Marine Life, Major Study Shows," *The Guardian*, December 10, 2009. Copyright © 2009 by *The Guardian*. All rights reserved. Reproduced by permission.

Irreversible Damage

A report by more than 100 of Europe's leading marine scientists, released at the climate talks this morning [December 10, 2009], states that the seas are absorbing dangerous levels of carbon dioxide as a direct result of human activity. This is already affecting marine species, for example by interfering with whale navigation and depleting planktonic species at the base of the food chain.

Ocean acidification—The facts say that acidity in the seas has increased 30% since the start of the industrial revolution. Many of the effects of this acidification are already irreversible and are expected to accelerate, according to the scientists.

The study, which is a massive review of existing scientific studies, warns that if CO_2 [carbon dioxide] emissions continue unchecked many key parts of the marine environment—particularly coral reefs and the algae and plankton which are essential for fish such as herring and salmon—will be "severely affected" by 2050, leading to the extinction of some species.

Dr Helen Phillips, chief executive of Natural England, which co-sponsored the report, said: "The threat to the delicate balance of the marine environment cannot be overstated—this is a conservation challenge of unprecedented scale and highlights the urgent need for effective marine management and protection."

Although oceans have acidified naturally in the past, the current rate of acidification is so fast that it is becoming extremely difficult for species and habitats to adapt. "We're counting it in decades, and that's the real take-home message," said Dr John Baxter a senior scientist with Scottish Natural Heritage, and the report's co-author. "This is happening fast."

Species Are Threatened

The report, published by the EU [European Union]-funded European Project on Ocean Acidification, a consortium of 27

> ## Ocean Acidity Past and Future
>
> The ocean absorbs around 25% of atmospheric CO_2 derived from burning fossil fuels and land use changes, and this CO_2 dissolves in sea water to form carbonic acid. As we have emitted more and more CO_2 into the atmosphere the ocean has absorbed greater amounts at increasingly rapid rates. This is altering the system's ability to adjust to changes in CO_2 that naturally occur over the millennia, significantly changing the chemistry of the seas, and leading to progressive acidification.
>
> Since the beginning of the industrial revolution 250 years ago, sea water acidity has increased by 30%. It should be noted that increasing sea water acidity lowers the ocean's natural 'basic' or 'alkaline' status and unnaturally forces the acid-base balance of sea water towards acid. If this accelerates for the next four decades as forecasted, the consequential increase in ocean acidity will be greater than anything experienced in the past 21 million years. Future projections show that by 2060, seawater acidity could have increased by 120%. To the best of our knowledge, the current rate of change is many times faster than anything previously experienced in the last 55 million years.
>
> D.d'A Laffoley and J.M. Baxter, eds.,
Ocean Acidification: The Facts,
European Project on Ocean Acidification, 2009.

research institutes and environment agencies, states that the survival of a number of marine species is affected or threatened, in ways not recognised and understood until now. These species include:

- whales and dolphins, who will find it harder to navigate and communicate as the seas become "noisier".

Sound travels further as acidity increases. Noise from drilling, naval sonar and boat engines is already travelling up to 10% further underwater and could travel up to 70% further by 2050.

- brittle stars (*Ophiothrix fragilis*) produce fewer larvae because they need to expend more energy maintaining their skeletons in more acid seas. These larvae are a key food source for herring.

- tiny algae such as *Calcidiscus leptoporus* which form the basis of the marine food chain for fish such as salmon may be unable to survive.

- young clownfish will lose their ability to "smell" the *Anemone* species that they shelter in. Experiments show that acidification interferes with the species' ability to detect the chemicals that give "olfactory cues".

"The bottom line is the only way to slow this down or reverse it is aggressive and immediate cuts in CO_2."

The report predicts that the north Atlantic, north Pacific and Arctic seas—a crucial summer feeding ground for whales—will see the greatest degree of acidification. It says that levels of aragonite, the type of calcium carbonate which is essential for marine organisms to make their skeletons and shells, will fall worldwide. But because cold water absorbs CO_2 more quickly, the study predicts that levels of aragonite will fall by 60% to 80% by 2095 across the Northern Hemisphere.

"The bottom line is the only way to slow this down or reverse it is aggressive and immediate cuts in CO_2," said Baxter. "This is a very dangerous global experiment we're undertaking here."

Written for policy makers and political leaders, the document is being distributed worldwide, with 32,000 copies printed in five major languages including English, Chinese and Arabic. Every member of the US Congress, now struggling to agree on a binding policy on CO_2 emissions, will be sent a copy.

Congressman Brian Baird, a Democrat representative from Washington State, who championed a bill in Congress promoting US research on ocean acidification, said these findings would help counter climate change sceptics [skeptics], since acidification was easily and immediately measurable.

"The consequences of ocean acidification may be every bit as grave as the consequences of temperature increases," he said. "It's one thing to question a computer extrapolation, or say it snowed in Las Vegas last year, but to say basic chemistry doesn't apply is a real problem [for the sceptics]. I think the evidence is really quite striking."

VIEWPOINT 4

The Seriousness of Ocean Acidification Is Overstated

Matt Ridley

Matt Ridley is a British journalist, writer, and businessman, as well as the author of The Rational Optimist: How Prosperity Evolves. *In the following viewpoint, he argues that ocean acidification is not a serious danger. He says that the increases in acid levels reported and predicted are well within natural variation, and should not harm marine life. On the contrary, he says, many marine creatures may actually grow faster and healthier as greater amounts of carbon dioxide are dissolved in the water. Ridley concludes that scientists should concentrate more on serious problems such as overfishing rather than acidification.*

As you read, consider the following questions:

1. On what grounds does Ridley argue that acid rain was not a serious problem in the 1980s and 1990s?
2. What will the drop in ocean pH be by the end of the century, according to Ridley?
3. On what grounds does Ridley suggest that corals and other species may increase in growth as more carbon dioxide is dissolved in the water?

Matt Ridley, "Who's Afraid of Acid in the Ocean? Not Me," *The Times* (UK), November 4, 2010. Copyright © 2010 by *The Times* (UK). All rights reserved. Reproduced by permission.

Today in Beijing, an alliance of scientists called Oceans United will present the UN with a request for $5 billion a year to be spent on monitoring the oceans. High among their concerns is ocean acidification.

As global warming loses traction on the public imagination, environmental pressure groups have been cranking the engine on this "other carbon dioxide problem". "Time is running out", wrote two activists recently in *Scientific American*, "to limit acidification before it irreparably harms the food chain on which the world's oceans—and people—depend." The fear is that acidification stops shellfish, coral, plankton, lobsters and crabs from building their protective shells.

The trouble is, a shoal of new scientific papers points to the conclusion that this scare is based on faulty biochemical reasoning and exaggerated extrapolation.

We have been here before. In 1984 acid rain was the scare of the day. As science correspondent of the *Economist*, I wrote: "Forests are beginning to die at a catastrophic rate. One year ago, West Germany estimated that 8 per cent of its trees were in trouble. Now 34 per cent are . . . that forests are in trouble is now indisputable." Experts told me that all Germany's conifers would be gone by 1990 and the Ministry of the Interior said all forests would be gone by 2002.

Bunk. Acid rain did not kill forests. It did not even damage them. Forests thrived in Germany, Scandinavia and North America during the 1980s and 1990s, despite acid rain. I was a gullible idiot not to question the conventional wisdom I was being fed by those with vested interests in alarm.

> *This scare is based on faulty biochemical reasoning and exaggerated extrapolation.*

Talking of vested interests, the European Project on Ocean Acidification is now a consortium of more than 100 scientists from 27 institutes and 9 countries. This summer it funded 35 scientists to spend six weeks in the Arctic studying the problem, "assisted" by the Greenpeace ship *Esperanza*. Think how little incentive the scientists would have to say: "Sorry, lads, we realise it is not much of an issue after all."

Start with a few facts. The oceans are not acid but alkaline, with an average pH of about 8.15 (0–7 being acid, 7–14 being alkaline). But they vary both in space and over time, Arctic seas being less strongly alkaline than tropical, and some bays and reefs being actually acid because of underwater volcanic emissions. The dissolution of carbon dioxide in the oceans may lower the pH slightly to about 7.9 or 7.8 by the end of the century at the worst.

Environmentalists like to call this a 30 per cent increase in acidity, because it sounds more scary than a 0.3 point (out of 14) decrease in alkalinity, but no matter. It is still well within the bounds of normal variation.

There are lots of threats to the ecosystems of the oceans, from overfishing to nutrient runoff, but acidification is way down the list.

Enough numbers. Try chemistry. The scary reasoning rests on the argument that lower pH will mean less dissolved carbonate in the water. But a new paper from North Carolina proves what some scientists have long suspected, namely that corals and other species do not use carbonate as raw material to make their shells; they use bicarbonate. And dissolving carbon dioxide in water actually increases bicarbonate concentrations.

This may explain why study after study keeps finding that, far from depressing growth rates of marine organisms, higher but realistic levels of carbon dioxide either do not affect them or increase their growth rate. By far the most numerous calcifiers in the oceans are plankton called coccolithophores. There is now strong evidence that coccolithophores are growing faster and larger as a result of human carbon dioxide emissions. Stands to reason if they use bicarbonate.

Studies of oyster sperm, cuttlefish eggs, juvenile sea stars, coral polyps and krill all point to the same conclusion: Damage only occurs when carbon dioxide reaches ludicrous levels that are not expected for many centuries, if at all.

When I voiced some of these doubts in my latest book, I was accused of cherry-picking studies. So let's look at a "meta-analysis", a summary of relevant published studies. Iris Hendriks and Carlos Duarte, of the Spanish Council for Scientific Research, found that in 372 studies of 44 different marine species "there was no significant mean effect" from lower pH. They concluded that marine life is "more resistant to ocean acidification than suggested by pessimistic predictions" and that it "may not be the widespread problem conjured into the 21st century".

I had assumed the evidence for damage from ocean acidification must be strong because that is what the media kept saying. I am amazed by what I have found. Make no mistake: There are lots of threats to the ecosystems of the ocean, from overfishing to nutrient runoff, but acidification is way down the list. The attention deflects funds and action from greater threats. It is time that scientists had the courage to admit this.

VIEWPOINT 5

The Pacific Ocean's Garbage Patch Should Be Cleaned Up

Paul Van Slambrouck

Paul Van Slambrouck is a journalist who writes for the Christian Science Monitor. *In the following viewpoint, he discusses sailor and activist Mary Crowley, who is organizing fishermen to help clean up a large garbage patch in the Pacific Ocean. The garbage patch is a giant shoal of plastic debris in the northern Pacific that may cover more area than Texas. According to Slambrouck, Crowley hopes to collect and recycle the plastic.*

As you read, consider the following questions:

1. According to the NOAA, why is there no accurate estimate on the size or mass of the garbage patch?
2. How long did the *Kaisei* trawl the garbage patch, and what did it discover?
3. What did Peter Sutter and Crowley report finding in the area of the garbage patch three decades ago?

Mary Crowley would rather be at sea. But she's not. Instead, she is in a small conference room at a roadside Marriott in this landlocked town north of Sacramento.

Project Kaisei

Around her are mainly men, many with beards, and many with baseball caps pulled down low and arms crossed tight. They are listening. Many of them would also rather be at sea.

Paul Van Slambrouck, "A Passion to Clean Up the Pacific Ocean's Great 'Garbage Patch,'" *Christian Science Monitor*, May 10, 2010. Copyright © 2010 by *Christian Science Monitor*. Reproduced by permission of the author.

Can these wishes be joined? We shall see in the next month or so.

Ms. Crowley has long hair, a ruddy outdoor complexion, and a sincere manner. She wants to sail west in the next month or two, out to what is called the North Pacific Trash Gyre. Her goal is to start cleaning up the plastic trash that has leaped into social consciousness over the past couple of years.

And she is urging some of the independent fishermen meeting here for the annual gathering of the Western Fishboat Owners Association to join her, using their boats to haul back garbage.

Her goal is to start cleaning up the plastic trash that has leaped into social consciousness over the past couple of years.

Whether they do or not, and it seems possible some will, Crowley leaves little doubt she will set sail this spring [2010], regardless. That determination is bringing her cleanup effort, called Project Kaisei, attention and resources to combat what strikes many as an overwhelming problem.

"It's audacious because the scale is so intimidating," says Matt Tinning, a spokesman for the Ocean Conservancy in Washington, D.C., a nonprofit group that mounts an annual global volunteer effort to clean the world's beaches. "Project Kaisei has captured the public spotlight by shining a light on the problem."

A Lot of Plastic

The exact dimensions of the North Pacific Trash Gyre aren't known. Some say it's the largest concentration of plastic debris in the world, a huge plastic garbage patch estimated to be either the size of Texas or twice that size.

Either way, there is general agreement that there is lots of plastic out there. But it is not a solid or even semisolid mass, as might be suggested by some descriptions. Nor is there any real data on the exact volume.

"Due to the limited sample size, as well as a tendency for observing ships to explore only areas thought to concentrate debris, there is really no accurate estimate on the size or mass of the 'garbage patch' or any other concentrations of marine debris in the open ocean," according to NOAA, the US government's National Oceanic and Atmospheric Administration.

The exact dimensions of the North Pacific Trash Gyre aren't known. Some say it's the largest concentration of plastic debris in the world, a huge plastic garbage patch estimated to be either the size of Texas or twice that size.

But Crowley has all the proof she needs.

Last summer, her Project Kaisei launched a month-long expedition to the North Pacific Gyre. Its tall, majestic sailing ship, the *Kaisei*, was accompanied by the *New Horizon*, a vessel from the Scripps Institution of Oceanography in San Diego.

Given the vastness of the ocean, some of the graduate students heading the voyage for Scripps were prepared to find less debris than forecast. But after the voyage the Scripps team reported: "The plastic indeed was there in the gyre. And there was lots and lots of it."

The *Kaisei* covered 3,000 nautical miles from Aug. 4 to 31 [2009]. It conducted several surface trawls every day and night. Every trawl came up with plastics of various sizes, shapes, and colors.

The discovery disturbed Crowley, who had been in the area 30 years earlier as a sailor. A native of Illinois, she spent her formative years sailing on Lake Michigan. "I grew up with a vision of doing long-distance sailing," she says, recalling efforts as a youngster to convince her parents to "give up everything and just sail."

After college Crowley became involved in the boat delivery business and eventually boat chartering, which is still what she does from her offices in Sausalito, Calif. She is also an educator, one of the founders in 1979 of the Ocean Voyages Institute, a nonprofit organization dedicated to teaching the maritime arts and sciences.

Three decades ago, Crowley and Peter Sutter, a renowned San Francisco yachtsman and sailmaker, took the 33-foot sailboat *Spirit* into the North Pacific, not toward some distant shore but out to the equivalent of ocean wilderness. Their destination was the North Pacific Gyre.

Over four or five days in the becalmed mid-ocean, Crowley says, they saw only a handful of pieces of plastic and one small abandoned fishing net.

Fast-forward to 2009, and Crowley's alarm at the concentration of trash she found last summer is understandable.

Crowley wants to recycle the plastic, not just relocate the trash onshore.

The Problem Can Be Solved

Yet as she sits in her Sausalito office with the San Francisco Bay visible over her shoulder, Crowley does not come across as an alarmist. "The big challenge for us is to get the word out that we do have the technology to figure out how to solve" this problem, she says.

She is raising money and enlisting support for a two-month expedition this summer, costing about $1.7 million. She envisions a small flotilla comprising a couple of fishing boats, a tug or marine supply ship, a barge, and the *Kaisei*.

John Varel, founder and CEO of FusionStorm, which provides back-end technology for businesses, has kicked in $100,000. Mr. Varel has started the FusionStorm Foundation to address ocean pollution.

The Great Pacific Garbage Patch

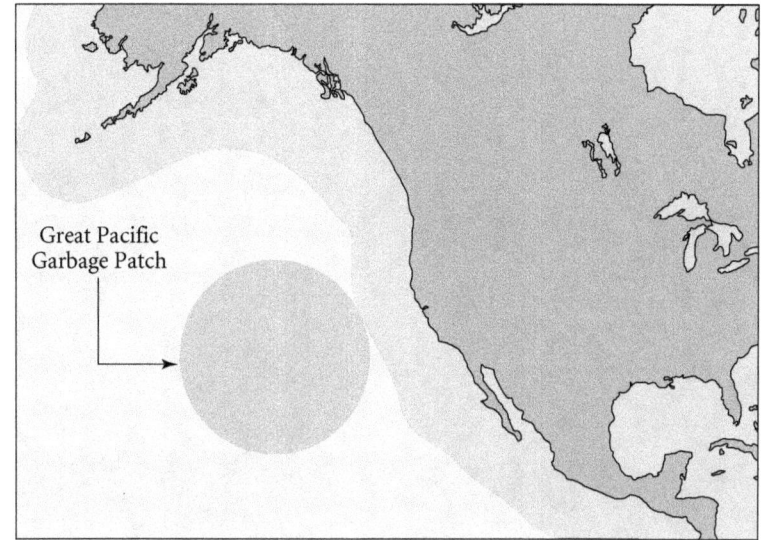

TAKEN FROM: "The Great Pacific Garbage Patch," Ocean Conservancy. http://act.oceanconservancy.org.

He was impressed with Crowley's solution-oriented attitude. "I was looking for someone who wanted to take this from the activist stage to the execution stage," he says.

Crowley wants to recycle the plastic, not just relocate the trash onshore. She knows there are no quick fixes here and that any cleanup needs to be combined with tougher maritime laws, as well as tougher recycling laws on the mainland to curtail the flow of garbage. Some 60 to 80 percent of the plastic in oceans is not released by ships but originates onshore before being swept out to sea via coastal waterways.

Enormous questions remain about the best ways to collect ocean plastics without harming sea life. Large fine-mesh nets might do the job, but would also scoop up marine creatures.

But Crowley doesn't seem overwhelmed.

"We want to make this everyone's problem, and everyone's solution," she tells the fishermen meeting in Rocklin.

VIEWPOINT 6

Cleaning Up the Plastic in the Oceans Will Accomplish Little

Richard Grant

Richard Grant is a British travel writer and the author of American Nomads: Travels with Lost Conquistadors, Mountain Men, Cowboys, Indians, Hoboes, Truckers, and Bullriders. *In the following viewpoint, he reports that plastic is omnipresent in the world's oceans, far outweighing the amount of plankton in the seas. There are so many plastic particles—many of them minuscule—that cleaning up the plastic is near impossible. Instead, plastic manufacturers need to start making plastic that is reusable, and people need to start recycling plastic and using less of it.*

As you read, consider the following questions:

1. How was the Great Pacific Garbage Patch discovered and by whom, according to Richard Grant?
2. How does Grant say that plastic kills seabirds and other ocean wildlife?
3. According to Grant, where does most marine plastic debris end up?

Way out in the Pacific Ocean, in an area once known as the doldrums, an enormous, accidental monument to modern society has formed. Invisible to satellites, poorly un-

Richard Grant, "Drowning in Plastic: The Great Pacific Garbage Patch Is Twice the Size of France," *The Telegraph*, April 24, 2009. Copyright © 2009 Telegraph Media Group Limited. Reproduced by permission.

derstood by scientists and perhaps twice the size of France, the Great Pacific Garbage Patch is not a solid mass, as is sometimes imagined, but a kind of marine soup whose main ingredient is floating plastic debris.

More Plastic than Plankton

It was discovered in 1997 by a Californian sailor, surfer, volunteer environmentalist and early-retired furniture restorer named Charles Moore, who was heading home with his crew from a sailing race in Hawaii, at the helm of a 50ft [foot] catamaran that he had built himself.

> *Fifty years ago nearly all that flotsam was biodegradable. These days it is 90 per cent plastic.*

For the hell of it, he decided to turn on the engine and take a shortcut across the edge of the North Pacific Subtropical Gyre, a region that seafarers have long avoided. It is a perennial high-pressure zone, an immense slowly spiralling vortex of warm equatorial air that pulls in winds and turns them gently until they expire. Several major sea currents also converge in the gyre and bring with them most of the flotsam from the Pacific coasts of Southeast Asia, North America, Canada and Mexico. Fifty years ago nearly all that flotsam was biodegradable. These days it is 90 per cent plastic.

'It took us a week to get across and there was always some plastic thing bobbing by,' says Moore, who speaks in a jaded, sardonic drawl that occasionally flares up into heartfelt oratory. 'Bottle caps, toothbrushes, Styrofoam cups, detergent bottles, pieces of polystyrene packaging and plastic bags. Half of it was just little chips that we couldn't identify. It wasn't a revelation so much as a gradual sinking feeling that something was terribly wrong here. Two years later I went back with a fine-mesh net, and that was the real mind-boggling discovery.'

Floating beneath the surface of the water, to a depth of 10 metres, was a multitude of small plastic flecks and particles, in many colours, swirling like snowflakes or fish food. An awful thought occurred to Moore and he started measuring the weight of plastic in the water compared to that of plankton. Plastic won, and it wasn't even close. 'We found six times more plastic than plankton, and this was just colossal,' he says. 'No one had any idea this was happening, or what it might mean for marine ecosystems, or even where all this stuff was coming from.'

So ended Moore's retirement. He turned his small volunteer environmental monitoring group into the Algalita Marine Research Foundation, enlisted scientists, launched public awareness campaigns and devoted all his considerable energies to exploring what would become known as the Great Pacific Garbage Patch and studying the broader problem of marine plastic pollution, which is accumulating in all the world's oceans.

Mermaids' Tears

The world's navies and commercial shipping fleets make a significant contribution, he discovered, throwing some 639,000 plastic containers overboard every day, along with their other litter. But after a few more years of sampling ocean water in the gyre and near the mouths of Los Angeles streams, and comparing notes with scientists in Japan and Britain, Moore concluded that 80 per cent of marine plastic was initially discarded on land, and the United Nations Environment Programme agrees.

The wind blows plastic rubbish out of littered streets and landfills, and lorries and trains on their way to landfills. It gets into rivers, streams and storm drains and then rides the tides and currents out to sea. Litter dropped by people at the beach is also a major source.

Plastic does not biodegrade; no microbe has yet evolved that can feed on it. But it does photodegrade. Prolonged exposure to sunlight causes polymer chains to break down into smaller and smaller pieces, a process accelerated by physical friction, such as being blown across a beach or rolled by waves. This accounts for most of the flecks and fragments in the enormous plastic soup at the becalmed heart of the Pacific, but Moore also found a fantastic profusion of uniformly shaped pellets about 2mm [millimetres] across.

'On Kamilo Beach in Hawaii there are now more plastic particles than sand particles until you dig a foot down.'

Nearly all the plastic items in our lives begin as these little manufactured pellets of raw plastic resin, which are known in the industry as nurdles. More than 100 billion kilograms of them are shipped around the world every year, delivered to processing plants and then heated up, treated with other chemicals, stretched and moulded into our familiar products, containers and packaging.

During their loadings and unloadings, however, nurdles have a knack for spilling and escaping. They are light enough to become airborne in a good wind. They float wonderfully and can now be found in every ocean in the world, hence their new nickname: mermaids' tears. You can find nurdles in abundance on almost any seashore in Britain, where litter has increased by 90 per cent in the past 10 years, or on the remotest uninhabited Pacific islands, along with all kinds of other plastic confetti.

'There's no such thing as a pristine sandy beach any more,' Charles Moore says. 'The ones that look pristine are usually groomed, and if you look closely you can always find plastic particles. On Kamilo Beach in Hawaii there are now more plastic particles than sand particles until you dig a foot down. On Pagan Island [between Hawaii and the Philippines] they have what they call the "shopping beach". If the islanders need a cigarette lighter, or some flip-flops, or a toy, or a ball for their kids, they go down to the shopping beach and pick it out of all the plastic trash that's washed up there from thousands of miles away.'

On Midway Island, 2,800 miles west of California and 2,200 miles east of Japan, the British wildlife filmmaker Rebecca Hosking found that many thousands of Laysan albatross chicks are dying every year from eating pieces of plastic that their parents mistake for food and bring back for them.

Deadly Plastic

Worldwide, according to the United Nations Environment Programme, plastic is killing a million seabirds a year, and 100,000 marine mammals and turtles. It kills by entanglement, most commonly in discarded synthetic fishing lines and nets. It kills by choking throats and gullets and clogging up digestive tracts, leading to fatal constipation. Bottle caps, pocket combs, cigarette lighters, tampon applicators, cotton bud shafts, toothbrushes, toys, syringes and plastic shopping bags are routinely found in the stomachs of dead seabirds and turtles.

A study of fulmar [a kind of seabird] carcasses that washed up on North Sea coastlines found that 95 per cent had plastic in their stomachs—an average of 45 pieces per bird.

Plastic particles are not thought to be toxic themselves but they attract and accumulate chemical poisons already in the water such as DDT and PCBs—nurdles have a special knack for this. Plastic has been found inside zooplankton and filter feeders such as mussels and barnacles; the worry is that these plastic pellets and associated toxins are travelling through the marine food chains into the fish on our plates. Scientists don't know because they are only just beginning to study it.

We do know that whales are ingesting plenty of plastic along with their plankton, and that whales have high concentrations of DDT, PCBs and mercury in their flesh, but that's not proof. The whales could be getting their toxins directly from the water or by other vectors.

Research on marine plastic debris is still in its infancy and woefully underfunded, but we know that there are six major subtropical gyres in the world's oceans—their combined area amounts to a quarter of the earth's surface—and that they are all accumulating plastic soup.

The Great Pacific Garbage Patch has now been tentatively mapped into an east and west section and the combined weight of plastic there is estimated at three million tons and increasing steadily. It appears to be the big daddy of them all, but we do not know for sure.

Dr Pearn Niiler of the Scripps [Institution of Oceanography] in San Diego, the world's leading authority on ocean currents, thinks that there is an even bigger garbage patch in the South Pacific, in the vicinity of Easter Island, but no scientists have yet gone to look.

Worldwide ... plastic is killing a million seabirds a year, and 100,000 marine mammals and turtles.

Plastic Everywhere

The French cultural theorist Paul Virilio observed that every new technology opens the possibility for a new form of accident. By inventing the locomotive, you also invent derailments. By inventing the aeroplane, you create plane crashes and midair collisions.

When Leo Baekeland, a Belgian chemist, started tinkering around in his garage in Yonkers, New York, working on the first synthetic polymer, who could have foreseen that a hundred years later plastic would outweigh plankton six-to-one in the middle of the Pacific Ocean? . . .

Except for the small percentage that has been incinerated, every single molecule of plastic that has ever been manufactured is still somewhere in the environment, and some 100 million tons of it are floating in the oceans.

Look around you. Start counting things made of plastic and don't forget your buttons, the stretch in your underwear, the little caps on the end of your shoelaces. The stuff is absolutely ubiquitous, forming the most basic infrastructure of modern consumer society. We are scarcely out of the womb when we meet our first plastic: wristband, aspirator, thermometer, disposable nappy. We gnaw on plastic teething rings and for the rest of our lives scarcely pass a moment away from plastics.

The benefits of plastic, most of which relate to convenience, consumer choice and profit, have been phenomenal. But except for the small percentage that has been incinerated, every single molecule of plastic that has ever been manufactured is still somewhere in the environment, and some 100 million tons of it are floating in the oceans.

A dead albatross was found recently with a piece of plastic from the 1940s in its stomach. Even if plastic production halted tomorrow, the planet would be dealing with its environmental consequences for thousands of years, and on the bottom of the oceans, where an estimated 70 per cent of marine plastic debris ends up—water bottles sink fairly quickly—for tens of thousands of years. It may form a layer in the geological record of the planet, or some microbe may evolve that can digest plastic and find itself supplied with a vast food resource. In the meantime, what can we do?

Cleanup Will Not Work

What we cannot do is clean up the plastic in the oceans. 'It's the biggest misunderstanding people have on this issue,' Moore says. They think the ocean is like a lake and we can go out with nets and just clean it up. People find it difficult to grasp the true size of the oceans and the fact that most of this plastic is in tiny pieces and it's everywhere. All we can do is stop putting more of it in, and that means redesigning our relationship with plastic.

At the far end of a huge loading warehouse on the San Francisco docks dub reggae is pulsing and two young women are shooting dry ice into two-litre plastic bottles. David de Rothschild, the tall, bearded, long-haired, environmentalist son of the Rothschild banking family, wearing hemp Nikes and a skull-and-bones belt buckle, strides in past a display of nurdles, an aquarium full of plastic soup and various rejected prototypes of the catamaran he intends to build and sail across the Pacific to Australia, visiting the Great Pacific Garbage Patch and various rubbish-strewn islands along the way.

What we cannot do is clean up the plastic in the oceans.

He wants the boat to be made entirely out of recycled plastics and float on recycled plastic bottles, and this has presented a daunting challenge to his team of designers, consultants and naval architects. Human ingenuity has devised many fine applications for recycled plastic, but boat-building has not so far been one of them. The design team has had to start from scratch, over and over again. Furthermore, because the point of this voyage is to galvanise media and public attention on the issue of plastic waste, the boat needs to look dramatic and iconic, and it must produce all its own energy, generate no emissions and compost its waste.

'The message of this project is that plastic's not the enemy,' de Rothschild says, speaking rapidly and unstoppably in a mid-Atlantic accent. He is full of bright energy, good humour, marketing slogans and an almost childlike enthusiasm. 'It's about rethinking waste as a resource. It's about doing smart things with plastic and showcasing solutions. It's about using adventure to engage people and start a conversation that creates change in society. You're always going to get people who say, "Oh, he's a bloody Rothschild, sitting on a boat made of, what's that? Champagne bottles?" And that's fine because it gets people talking about it and thinking about where their rubbish goes.' . . .

He decided to name the boat *Plastiki*, in homage to *Kon-Tiki*, the raft of balsa logs and hemp ropes in which Thor Heyerdahl sailed across the Pacific in 1947. He recruited designers, a public relations team and corporate sponsors, including Hewlett-Packard and the International Watch Company. He won't say how much it is costing or how much of his own money is going into it, only that it is more than he would like and less than it could be. . . .

Design for Reuse

In general terms, it is already clear what we need to do about plastic. Since it is made from oil, which will run out in our lifetimes and get more expensive as it does, we have to start reusing plastic and designing it for reuse. At present only a few of our many hundred plastics can simply be melted down and moulded into something else; the rest are cross-contaminated with other chemicals and types of plastic. But the billion-dollar plastic industry is tooled for virgin plastic and resistant to change.

Charles Moore gives talks to plastic industry executives whenever he can and finds very little interest in recycling, because it's the least profitable sector of the industry. 'A lot of companies and product designers and marketing people don't like recycled plastic either,' de Rothschild says, 'You can't dye it with those bright, attention-grabbing colours.'

For consumers, the easiest way to make a difference is to give up plastic shopping bags and plastic water bottles, which contribute more to plastic pollution than any other products. Then comes plastic packaging, which is a little more complicated. It is easy to point out examples of excessive packaging, but plastic does have the virtue of being lighter than paper, cardboard and glass, which gives it a smaller carbon footprint. For food especially, recyclable plastic packaging is probably the best option.

We have to start reusing plastic and designing it for reuse.

For the hull and cabin of the *Plastiki*, the team was enthused about recycled plastic lumber until they discovered that it sags badly unless reinforced with glass rods. Now they are excited about self-reinforcing PET, a new product manufactured in Denmark, similar to fibreglass but fully recycled and recyclable. When heat-fused to boards of PET foam, it appears to be capable of withstanding the battering of Pacific waves for a hundred days, although the effect of salt water on the material is still unknown. Dry ice in the two-litre bottles hardens them without losing any flotation, although some of the bottle caps have managed to work themselves loose and are now being resealed with what de Rothschild calls 'a very cool bio-glue' made from cashew nuts and sugar.

Sitting now with a pint of beer and an artichoke in a restaurant opposite the waterfront, he is confident that the *Plastiki* will be built and on its way to Australia sometime this summer. 'We do need to get from A to B but what this project is really about is remarketing and rebranding the message about recycling, about sustainability, about interconnectedness,' he says. What he sees as the failure of the environmental movement, as measured by ever-increasing carbon emissions, rain forest destruction, species extinctions and marine plastic debris, he understands as a failure of marketing and communication, rather than insurmountable forces working in the opposite direction.

'The environmental message has been very exclusive, very guilt-mongering, very fear-mongering, and is that the right way to engage with people? We're bombarded by 2,500 images a day. How are you going to stop someone watching *Lost* [a television series] and make them watch someone saying, "You're a bad person because you don't drive a hybrid"? To effect change, you've got to inspire people, not moan at them.'

After another pint, he admits to serious doubts—not that the *Plastiki* will get built and complete its voyage, but that it is still possible to save the oceans from ecological collapse. Overfishing is the most urgent problem, but what really scares him and the marine scientists is acidification caused by global warming. The oceans are absorbing more and more of the carbon dioxide that we are putting into the air and it is changing the pH of the water, turning the seas more acid, with potentially catastrophic effects on marine organisms and ecosystems.

'A lot of scientists think we're basically screwed, but what are you going to do?' he asks. 'Enjoy your beer, enjoy your family, make the most of it while it lasts? I think there's a real big movement for that at the moment and part of me understands that. But there's a bigger part of me that says we've got to find a solution, collectively. I mean, come on. We spent $265 billion preparing for the Y2K bug [referring to a potential problem with computers at the beginning of the year 2000] and we didn't even know if it was going to happen or not. We know for an absolute fact that if we continue on our current rate of consumption, we're going to run out of resources. But the annual budget for the United Nations Environment Programme last year was $190 million. And the budget for the latest James Bond movie was $205 million.'

He chuckles at that, checks his watch and calls for the bill. It is time to walk the dogs and then work the second half of his standard 17-hour day. Outside, he points to San Francisco Bay, looking pristine and lovely in the late afternoon sunshine. 'Maybe that's the trouble,' he says. 'You'd never guess what's under the surface if you didn't know, would you?'

Periodical and Internet Sources Bibliography

The following articles have been selected to supplement the diverse views presented in this chapter.

Renee Cho	"Our Oceans: A Plastic Soup," *State of the Planet* (blog), January 26, 2011. http://blogs.ei.columbia.edu.
Economist	"A Sinking Feeling," March 12, 2009.
P. Gosselin	"Ocean Acidification Doesn't Lead to Species Die-Off, Surprising Scientists," *NoTricksZone* (blog), July 26, 2010. http://notrickszone.com.
Scott Learn	"Reports of Pacific Ocean's Plastic Patch Being Texas-Sized Are Grossly Exaggerated, Oregon State University Professor Says," *Oregonian*, January 4, 2011.
Michael D. Lemonick	"The Secret of Sea Level Rise: It Will Vary Greatly by Region," *Yale Environment 360*, March 22, 2010.
Bjorn Lomborg	"Cost-Effective Ways to Address Climate Change," *Washington Post*, November 17, 2010.
Phil Mercer	"W Australia Sea Level Rising Fast," BBC News, November 9, 2009. www.bbc.co.uk.
Patrick J. Michaels	"Don't Boo-Hoo for Tuvalu," Cato Institute, November 10, 2001. www.cato.org.
National Resources Defense Council	"Ocean Acidification: The Other CO2 Problem," September 17, 2009. www.nrdc.org.
Joseph Romm	"Lomborg Misrepresents Possible Sea-Level Rise," *Grist*, September 15, 2007.
Emily Sohn	"Mystery of the Missing Ocean Plastic," Discovery News, August 19, 2010. http://news.discovery.com.

CHAPTER 2

Managing Water Scarcity

VIEWPOINT 1

Climate Shifts and Human Action Have Caused Irreversible Desertification in the Sahel

Alex Shoumatoff

Alex Shoumatoff is senior contributing editor to Vanity Fair *and author of* The World Is Burning: Murder in the Rain Forest. *In the following viewpoint, he reports that the Sahel region in Africa is being irreversibly turned into desert. Part of the problem, he says, is overpopulation and the resulting clearing of land for firewood. With trees gone, the soil degrades and the land turns to desert. However, Shoumatoff notes, global warming and global climate change have also affected the region, resulting in more severe drought. Shoumatoff concludes that the rest of the world may eventually experience desertification just as the Sahel is.*

As you read, consider the following questions:

1. According to Shoumatoff, where around the earth has Sahara dust been blown?
2. What does Shoumatoff say are the two schools of thought about the causes of desertification?
3. What is China doing to slow desertification, and how effective are its efforts, according to Shoumatoff?

Alex Shoumatoff, "The Desertification of Mali," dispatchesfromthevanishingworld.com, January 10, 2006. Copyright © 2006 by Alex Shoumatoff. All rights reserved. Reproduced by permission.

63

Water

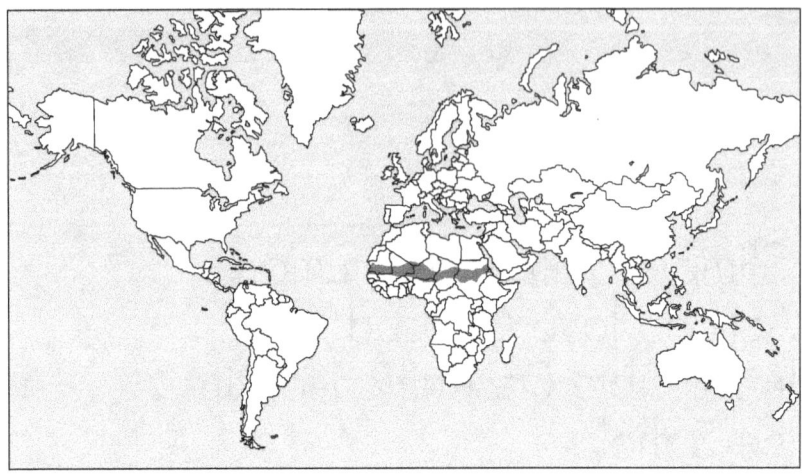

Five of the ten days I was in Mali last March [2005], I never saw the sun. It was blotted out by an epic dust cloud that spread hundreds of miles in every direction, borne by the harmattan, the southwesterly gale that blows down from the Sahara during the dry season. Sandstorms have always been a part of life here. They can be so thick you can't even see your hand.

Drought and Deforestation

Historically, the harmattan blows in December through February. But since 1968 Mali and the rest of the Sahel (the semi-arid band below the Sahara and above the humid savannas and forests to the south, that stretches from Senegal to Eritrea) have been experiencing a prolonged, devastating drought. Precipitation has dropped 30 percent—the most dramatic decline on earth—and the rainy season has been truncated to two months, July and August.

At the same time, the population of the Sahel ("shore" in Arabic) has been exploding, compounding the demand for firewood, the main source of cooking fuel. A million acres of trees a year are being cleared and burned in Mali alone. Both these things—the drought, amplified by the deforestation—

have brought catastrophic desertification to the Sahel. The sandstorms have increased tenfold since 1968. They pick up an estimated two to three billion tons of Sahara sand and dust a year and now can come any time from September to June. The finest red particles are whipped up into the upper atmosphere, to 12,000 feet and higher, and are transported across oceans by the prevailing winds. In January 2004, cars in Florida and South Texas were coated with Sahara dust.

In June [2005] a similar "blood rain" fell in England. In February the sun was blotted out in Austria. NASA [National Aeronautics and Space Administration] satellite photos showed a cloud larger than Spain off the coast of Morocco. Sahara dust travels to Toronto and even Greenland. It is snuffing coral reefs and sea urchins in the Caribbean. So the Sahel's desertification is not just a matter of local concern.

Both these things—the drought, amplified by the deforestation—have brought catastrophic desertification to the Sahel.

During the first five years of the drought, until 1973, 250,000 people and 3.5 million head of cattle in the Sahel died. In 1984–5 rural Mali (a parched, land-locked country nearly twice the size of Texas whose top two-thirds—from Timbuktu north—are in the Sahara, and whose bottom third is in the Sahel) again became uninhabitable, and many of the villages, where three-quarters of the population live, were vacated. Most of the environmental refugees poured into Bamako, the capital, whose population has grown from 800,000 to two million in the last 20 years.

In 2003, the first good rains in 50 years fell, and 2004 was also a relatively wet year. But the rains triggered the emergence of billions of pink African desert locusts, which skeletonized whatever vegetation they landed on. In Niger, the next country to the east, where the rural population was al-

Water

ready at the edge after three decades of drought, the scourge last summer produced a famine of Ethiopian direness. This year, too, the rains would be good, but there were still these epic sandstorms before they came. The drought may have subsided for now, but most scientists are in agreement that the processes that are desertifying the Sahel have reached the point where they are unstoppable.

Deforestation Exacerbates Climate Change

Bamako, where my quest to understand these processes began, sprawls unprepossessingly on both sides of the Niger River. Few houses are more than one story. The city seems more like a big village, an anarchic collection of bougous, or neighborhoods, where Mali's various ethnic groups live in vast extended families—the Bamana with the Bamana, the Songhai with the Songhai, the Peul with the Peul. The women cook on charcoal braziers in the courtyards. The charcoal smoke mingles with the diesel fumes and the Sahara dust, so the pall over Bamako was particularly thick.

The latest United Nations Human Development report (released in 2003) ranks Mali as the 184th worst country in the world out of 187 to be living in terms of its annual per capita income ($350), mean education level (fourth grade), average life span (49), and infant mortality rate (119 out of 1000 live births). Yet Mali's art—particularly its music and wood sculpture—ranks high among the world's cultural treasures. And perhaps because there is so little to steal, there is very little crime in the country's Sahel region (although there are Islamist terrorists and bandits in the north). Its government, though cash-strapped, is one of Africa's most promising new democracies. Many families have a member in New York or Paris who wires home money, which bolsters the actual economic picture. But many villages are barely surviving.

Managing Water Scarcity

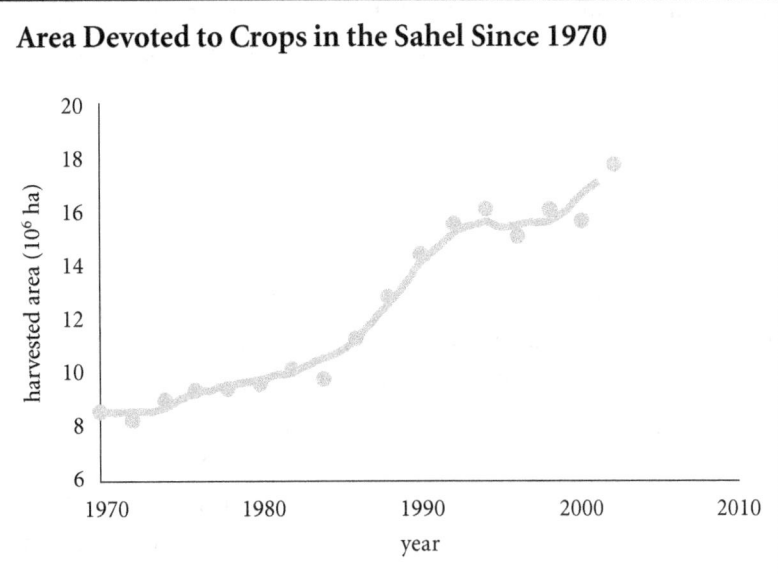

Area Devoted to Crops in the Sahel Since 1970

As more crops were needed, agriculture spread into areas poorly suited for crops, resulting in land degradation in dry years.
Based on data from United Nations Environment Programme, World Agroforestry Centre, "Climate Change and Variability in the Sahel Region: Impacts and Adaptation Strategies in the Agricultural Sector."

TAKEN FROM: Robert Stewart, "Desertification in the Sahel," Ocean World, 2008. http://oceanworld.tamu.edu.

There are two schools of thought about the desertification, I discovered. The "degradation narrative," as it is referred to by one of its critics, was first proposed during the Ethiopian famine of 1972–4, which actually gripped the entire Sahel and was run by the media. It attributed the desertification to rampant deforestation, which is still going on: When the trees go, the grass below them dies; then the ground dries up, the soil blows away (adding to the dust in the atmosphere) and any remaining condensation in the soil is evaporated or runs off immediately. The other school, drawing on recent studies of climate data, attributes desertification primarily to "the remote influence"—a cyclical shift in the world's climate, exacerbated by the accumulation of greenhouse gases warming the earth's atmosphere. In fact both factors are involved. The remote influence is the main cause, but it is enhanced by deforestation.

> *"Malians have always had droughts to contend with. . . . But now there is also the problem of overpopulation."*

One morning, I went to the Sahel Institute, which was founded in 1973, after the first famine took a quarter of a million lives. Its members consist of the eight Sahel countries (Mali, Niger, Burkina Faso, Chad, Gambia, Mauritania, and Senegal) and Cabo Verde, the island out in the Atlantic, which is desertifying because the Sahara's dust clouds are suppressing the winds that bring it rain. I was taken down a dark, empty corridor the length of a football field to the office of Dr. Boubacar Diallo, the institute's economist and coordinator of food security, who laid out the degradation narrative.

"Malians have always had droughts to contend with," he explained in such calm, measured tones that a listener could be forgiven for not grasping the gravity of the situation. "There were droughts 10,000 years ago and in the 13th century that made the Sahel uninhabitable. But now there is also the problem of overpopulation.

Overpopulation

The Sahel's population is currently 50 million and is growing by 2.7 percent a year. By 2050 it will conservatively hit 100 million. This is because the women continue to have seven children. Before there was equilibrium because of infant mortality and sickness, but now, with the availability of modern medicine, demographic growth is unchecked.

"For the people in the villages," he went on, "wood is the only fuel and the only source of income, and the forest also provides traditional plant medicines, the first line of defense against disease.

"So there is a lot of harvesting. And in Bamako almost everybody cooks with charcoal, which produces only one-third of the energy that raw wood does [though it is lighter and more portable, and easier to ignite]. So abandoning the countryside doesn't alleviate the deforestation. It actually accelerates it."

> "Global climate patterns are implicated. The whole world is slowly becoming a desert. That is why everyone should be concerned about what is happening here. This is the future."

The institute tried to "politicize" the villagers: "We showed them pictures of what it was like 30 years ago and now, so they could see the degradation," Dr. Diallo explained. "But it hasn't worked. They keep cutting and having lots of children. The same piece of land that used to feed five people now has to feed 20, and it has deteriorated, so the farmers"—pretty much every village grows its own food—"are venturing into more and more marginal, waterless land." The institute was now concentrating on raising the productivity of the land already under cultivation, by introducing new, improved strains of millet and other crops, fertilizers, and anti-erosion and water-retention techniques. This slowed down the clearing for farming, but it didn't stop the clearing for firewood.

"Stopping the desertification is impossible," Dr. Diallo concluded. "All we can do is try to slow it down.

"It isn't caused only by local deforestation. Global climate patterns are implicated. The whole world is slowly becoming a desert. That is why everyone should be concerned about what is happening here. This is the future."

According to the United Nations Environment Programme, half of the world's land surface—28 million of its 57 million square miles—is "dryland": plains, grasslands, savannas, steppes, or pampas with a modest water supply compared to the world's forests.

Four million square miles are hyperarid desert, and another 19 million are becoming desert or are threatened with desertification. Desertification is proceeding worldwide at a faster rate than any other time in recorded history, with disastrous effects for vegetative cover, biodiversity, and the existence of 1.5 billion people in more than 100 countries. Twenty-seven percent of China is desert, and the country's Gobi and Taklimakan deserts are expanding at a rate of 2,800 square miles a year, despite the most massive tree-planting campaign ever undertaken (42 billion trees have been planted by 560 million people since 1982). And so what is happening in the Sahel is a frightening model, an advanced case of what much of the earth's surface is going to turn into.

VIEWPOINT 2

Human Action Is Reversing Desertification in the Sahel

Mae-Wan Ho and Lim Li Ching

Mae-Wan Ho is a retired British geneticist and author of The Rainbow and the Worm: The Physics of Organisms; *Lim Li Ching is the London-based deputy editor of the quarterly magazine* Science in Society. *In the following viewpoint, the authors argue that the desertification of the Sahel was due to normal climate variation, not to overpopulation or deforestation. In fact, the authors argue, the inhabitants of the Sahel have not caused desertification, but are instead reversing it through careful farming practises and tree-planting initiatives. The authors conclude that greening efforts must be led by local farmers, not by outside scientists.*

As you read, consider the following questions:

1. What were the results of the droughts in the Sahel from the 1960s to the 1980s, according to the authors?
2. Why do the authors say that high local population densities are essential in the Sahel?
3. In what way did changing how trees were regarded by law benefit farmers and the environment in Niger, according to the authors?

Mae-Wan Ho and Lim Li Ching, "Greening the Desert," Institute of Science in Society, February 1, 2008. Copyright © 2008 by Institute of Science in Society. All rights reserved. Reproduced by permission.

Water

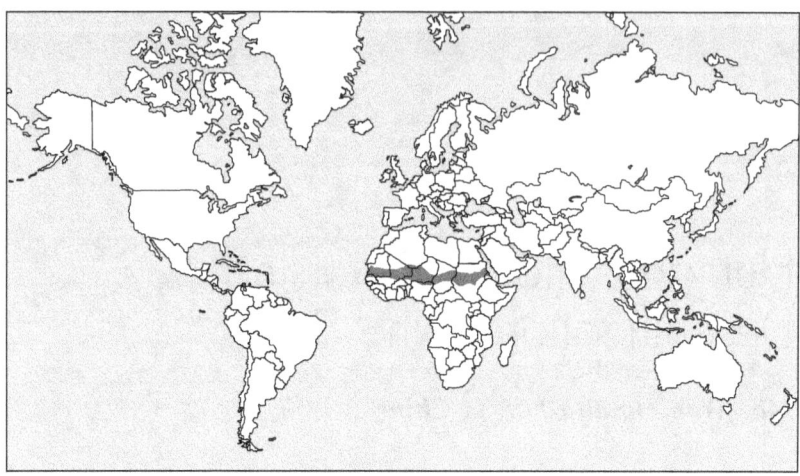

For years, many scientists have been making dire predictions of widespread irreversible "desertification" in the African Sahel. But recent findings have proven them wrong.

Reclaiming the Desert

Satellite images consistently show an increase in "greenness" since the 1980s over large areas, confirming evidence on the ground indicating that the Sahel has recovered from the great droughts of the 1980s, and that human factors have played a large role in reclaiming the desert.

The African Sahel is a semiarid grass and shrubland region situated between the Sahara desert in the north and the humid tropical savannas in the south, with a steep north-south gradient in mean annual rainfall. Rainfall is markedly seasonal and variable. A long dry season alternates with a short humid season during the Northern Hemisphere summer. The scarcity of rainfall and its variable, unpredictable pattern accentuating from south to north, are the most important factors that shape the Sahel ecosystem. The vegetation cycle closely corresponds to the seasonality in rainfall, with virtually all the plant growth in the humid summer months. Overlying the sharp seasonal contrasts in rainfall are considerable fluctuations from year to year, and from one decade to another.

Although variable rainfall and droughts are seen as normal in arid and semiarid climates, the droughts that struck the Sahel in the late 1960s through to the 1980s were unprecedented in length and severity. Land degradation and famine during the droughts, exacerbated by political instability and unrest, prompted the UN [United Nations] to hold a conference on desertification in 1977. This initiated a debate, still ongoing, on the causes and effects of drought, land degradation and desertification.

The Sahel has recovered from the great droughts of the 1980s.

There are two opposing camps in the debate. Adherents of the desertification hypothesis hold human activities responsible for "irreversible" declines in vegetation from "overuse of resources" and "human mismanagement". Sceptics [skeptics], however, see declines in vegetation as the result of drought, and hence a temporary phenomena, with humans playing only a minor role, if at all.

Some scientists have stressed the high potential of adaptation of the Sahel population to rainfall variability, and they are right....

Evidence Emerging from the Ground

Evidence of recovery has been coming from the ground since at least the beginning of the present century. Fred Pearce reported in the *New Scientist* in 2001 on how in Nigeria, Niger, Senegal, Burkina Faso and Kenya, integrated farming, mixed cropping and traditional soil and water conservation methods have been increasing per capita food production several fold, keeping well ahead of population growth.

The use of sheep manure for fertiliser gave increased yields for farmers in Kano, Nigeria. Planting leguminous crops increased nutrient levels in the soil by fixing nitrogen from the air. Integration of crops and livestock enhances nutrient cycling; legumes and manure return to the soil what crops take out. The Kano region is the most agriculturally productive part of the country, with increased yields of sorghum, millet, cowpeas and groundnuts.

A four-year study in eastern Burkina Faso challenged the assumption that land is degrading largely due to human activities. It found that despite declining rainfall since the late 1950s and increasing populations, there was no evidence of land degradation connected to human activities nor a decline in food productivity. Conversely, yields of many crops have risen, and there was no decline of soil fertility over 30 years.

These farmers did not achieve environmental sustainability through a capital-intensive or high-tech path. In Burkina Faso, the increased yields of sorghum, millet and groundnuts could hardly be attributable to increased external inputs, because these crops received little fertiliser and were cultivated largely with a hand hoe.

Despite declining rainfall since the late 1950s and increasing populations, there was no evidence of land degradation connected to human activities nor a decline in food productivity.

The scientists found that farmers have a rich repertoire of soil and water conservation technologies, such as crop sequencing, crop rotation, fallowing, weeding, selective clearing, intercropping, appropriate crop and landrace selection, plant spacing, thinning, mulching, stubble grazing, weeding mounds, paddocking, household refuse application, manure application, crop residue application and compost pits. Mechanical practises include perennial grass strips, stone lines, wood barriers, earth barriers, brick barriers, stalk barriers, stone bunds, earth bunds and living hedges.

Perhaps more important than the practises is the selective way they are used, which vary with different field types, allowing optimal adjustment of limited labour and inputs to the requirements of different crops and soils. If land becomes limited, farmers do not need to invent new management systems; they apply these soil and water conservation practises *more intensively*. Farmers also apply land management practises only when and where needed. Using their knowledge of crops and soils, they treat only the parts of their field that need particular attention at any one time.

High local population densities, far from being a liability, are actually essential for providing the necessary labour to work the land, dig terraces and collect water in ponds for irrigation, and to control weeds, tend fields, feed animals and spread manure. As population densities increase, farmers intensify their cooperation systems, grouping to tend each other's fields at busy periods, lending and borrowing land, livestock and equipment, and swapping seed varieties.

People thus invest heavily in creating and maintaining social networks that share land, labour, seeds, cattle grazing bushland, technologies and cash. These networks enhance the ability of farmers to farm sustainably and efficiently by cooperation and reciprocity. They also allow people to diversify their livelihoods, learn from each other, and minimise risks, thus avoiding poverty traps.

Furthermore, in Maradi district of southern Niger, where repeated droughts have wrought environmental damage, farmers have reversed the damages and reclaimed the desert. This was also true of Machakos (renamed Makueni) district of Kenya. In the 1930s, British colonial scientists had condemned the bare eroding hills of the drought-prone area to environmental oblivion; likewise the local Akamba people were seen

> ## Niger Reforested
>
> Recent studies of vegetation patterns, based on detailed satellite images and on-the-ground inventories of trees, have found that Niger, a place of persistent hunger and deprivation, has recently added minions of new trees and is now far greener than it was 30 years ago.
>
> These gains, moreover, have come at a time when the population of Niger has exploded, confounding the conventional wisdom that population growth leads to the loss of trees and accelerates land degradation, scientists studying Niger say.
>
>
>
> *Lydia Polgreen,*
> *"In Niger, Trees and Crops Turn Back the Desert,"*
> New York Times, *February 11, 2007. www.nytimes.com.*
>
>

as doomed to a miserable poverty-rife existence. The same narrative was consistently reproduced in the 1950s and 1970s. Yet researchers found the hills greener, less eroded and more productive than before, despite a fivefold population increase. The Akamba had responded to the droughts by switching from herding cattle to settled farming, giving them incentive to work the land effectively.

Trees Are Flourishing

In Niger today, millions of trees are flourishing, thanks to poor local farmers. There are at least 3 million tree-covered hectares, not the result of the large-scale planting or other expensive methods often advocated by African politicians and aid groups, but by the efforts of individual farmers themselves. The area is far greener than it was 30 years ago; and these gains have come at a time when the population of Niger has exploded.

How did all this come about? Lydia Polgreen told the story in the *Herald Tribune*. About 20 years ago, farmers like Ibrahim Danjimo realised something had to be done. "We look around, all the trees were far from the village," he said, "Suddenly, the trees were all gone."

Danjima, now in his 40s, has been working the rocky, sandy soil of his tiny village since he was a child. He and other farmers in Guidan Bakoye took a small but radical step of not clearing the saplings from their fields before planting as they had for generations. Instead, they would protect and nurture the saplings, carefully ploughing around them when sowing millet, sorghum, peanuts and beans.

The area is far greener than it was 30 years ago; and these gains have come at a time when the population of Niger has exploded.

Another change was the way trees were regarded by law. From colonial times, all trees in Niger had been property of the state, which gave farmers little incentive to protect them, and they were chopped for firewood or construction.

Over time, farmers began to regard the trees in their fields as their property, and in recent years, the government has recognised the benefits and allowed individuals to own trees. Farmers make money off trees by selling branches, pods, fruit and bark.

Mahamane Larwanou, a forestry expert at the University of Niamey in Niger's capital, said the revival of trees had transformed rural life. Farmers can sell the branches for money; they can feed the pods as fodder to their animals, sell or eat the leaves and fruits. The tree roots fix the soil in place, preventing it from being carried off with the fierce Sahel winds. The roots also help hold water in the ground rather than letting it run off into gullies that flood villages and destroy crops.

Wrestling subsistence for 13 million people from Niger's fragile ecology is something akin to a puzzle. Larwanou said, "Less than 12 percent of the country's land can be cultivated, and much of that is densely populated. Yet 90 percent of Niger's people live off agriculture, cultivating a semiarid strip along the southern edge of the country."

Farmers practise mostly rain-fed agriculture. The return of trees increases the income of rural farmers, cushioning them against the boom-and-bust cycle of farming and herding.

Ibrahim Idy, a farmer in Dahirou, a village in the Zinder region, has 20 baobab trees in his fields. Selling the leaves and fruit brings him about $300 a year in additional income. He has used that to buy a motorised pump that draws water from his well to irrigate his cabbage and lettuce fields, and sends his children to school. His neighbour, who has fewer baobab trees, cannot send his children to school; instead they have to draw water from the well. In some regions, swaths of land that had fallen out of use are being reclaimed with labour-intensive but inexpensive techniques.

In the village of Koloma Baba, in the Tahoua region just south of the desert's edge, a group of widows has reclaimed fields once thought forever barren. They dug pits in plots of land as hard as asphalt, placed a shovel of manure in each pit and wait for rain. The pits held the water and manure stayed in the soil and regenerated its fertility. In this way, more than 240,000 ha [hectare] of land have been reclaimed, according to researchers. But it is still a hand-to-mouth existence, the women produce enough to eat, and disaster is always just one missed rainfall away.

While Niger's experience of greening on a vast scale is unique, smaller tracts of land have been revived in other countries. "It really requires the effort of the whole community," said Larwanou. "If farmers don't take action themselves and the community doesn't support it, farmer-managed regeneration cannot work."

Moussa Bara, the chief of Dan Saga, a village in the Aguié region where the regeneration has been a huge success, said the village had benefited enormously from the revival of trees. He said not a single child had died of malnutrition in the hunger crisis that gripped Niger in 2005, largely because of extra income from selling firewood. Still, he said, the village has too many mouths to feed.

The greening of Sahel is a clear example of how the dominant Western knowledge system had grossly misinformed policy makers.

Underestimating Local Farmers

Chris Reij, now at the Free University Amsterdam in the Netherlands, presented the findings in Niger at the "From Desert to Oasis" symposium in Niamey. He wants to spread the success of Niger to neighbouring countries including Mali, Senegal and Burkina Faso. The programme will form part of the Oasis initiative to reclaim deserts, which was launched at the symposium in October 2006 by 11 African countries, with support from international research and government agencies.

Let's hope they will continue to let local farmers lead the projects, with scientists taking a supporting role. As Fred Pearce stressed of the Sahel miracle, "This is no high-tech breakthrough, nor a result of Western aid programmes." A major reason for the overestimation of land degradation is the underestimation of local farmers' abilities. Scientists, policy makers and aid workers must recognise the overriding importance of local knowledge and ingenuity for innovation, as well as the cooperative community networks for solving our problems of survival in times of climate change.

The greening of Sahel is a clear example of how the dominant Western knowledge system had grossly misinformed policy makers; and it was the knowledge and initiatives of local farmers that saved the situation.

VIEWPOINT 3

China's Water Crisis May Be Helped by Trading Water Rights

Zhou Jigang, Peng Guangcan, and Ceng Zhen

Zhou Jigang, Peng Guangcan, and Ceng Zhen are Chongqing-based journalists. In the following viewpoint, they report that China has been suffering from a severe water shortage. This has resulted in conflicts over access to water between different regions, the authors say. They note that China is having some success with solving these problems by setting up a market-based system for trading water rights. However, they conclude, administrative difficulties and competing interests mean that establishing effective water-trading regulations will be challenging.

As you read, consider the following questions:

1. According to the authors, what may have been China's first sale of water rights?
2. What do the authors say has spurred Tongliang to implement Chongqing's first regulations on water rights trading?
3. What does one need in order to achieve good results with pollution or water trading, according to the authors?

Zhou Jigang, Peng Guangcan, and Ceng Zhen, "Trading Water in Thirsty China," china dialogue.net, June 26, 2008. Copyright © 2010 by chinadialogue.net. All rights reserved. Reproduced by permission.

Managing Water Scarcity

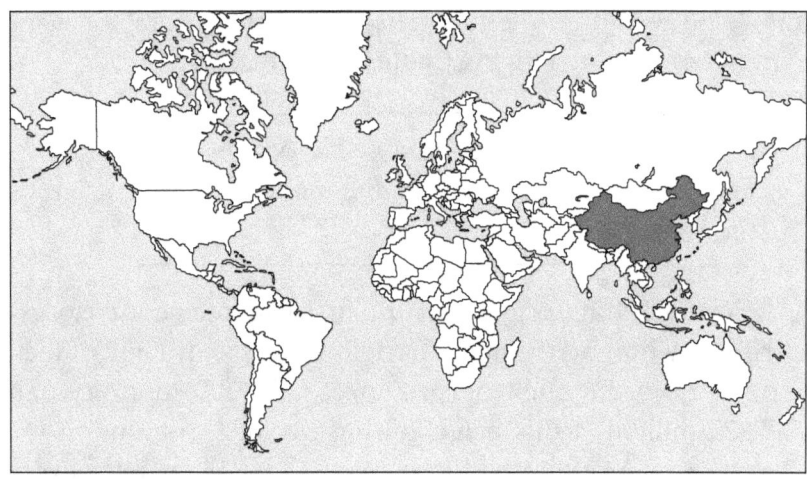

On April 1, 2008, the Tongliang county water authority in Chongqing, southwest China, approved Zhu Jiaping's application for water usage. With stamps from the town of Pulu and three villages within its borders, the document gave Zhu the legal right to use water from limestone caves at Xinlian village.

Salamanders and Water Trading

Zhu's company planned to use the water to raise giant salamanders. New regulations on the allocation of water rights in the county meant his application had to explain the potential impact of his company's water usage on local stakeholders. Liu Shangwu, a water management official, explained that three nearby villages had to agree that the application did not impact on their water security. Otherwise it would not have been approved.

The procedures were complicated, but Zhu believed it was worthwhile. A written agreement would give him a stronger position if there were future disputes over water abstraction. More importantly, it meant that if any firms moved into the nearby Tongliang Development Zone and wanted to take water from the same source, they would have to purchase it from him. Zhu would be the first person to benefit from the standardisation of water rights trading in China.

> *As the concept of carbon trading has become increasingly familiar in China, water trading has also appeared on the horizon.*

However, Tongliang is not the first Chinese county to experiment with water trading. Back in 2000, the drought-ridden city of Yiwu, in Zhejiang province, paid 200 million yuan (US$29 million) to its neighbouring city of Dongyang in exchange for 50 million cubic metres of drinking water every year in perpetuity. This may have been China's first sale of water rights. In 2006, the water authority in Beijing announced the city would pay 20 million yuan in "environmental compensation" to the neighbouring province of Hebei and purchase water from both Hebei and Shanxi province.

As the concept of carbon trading [that is, trading in the right to produce carbon emissions] has become increasingly familiar in China, water trading has also appeared on the horizon. Informal trading has become increasingly common, but Tongliang local government was the first to put these deals into a legal framework. One thing is for sure: This is only the start.

The Water Crisis

The underlying cause of such schemes is China's worsening water crisis. Since 1990, one-fifth of Chinese arable land has suffered from drought, according to state news agency Xinhua. Four hundred of China's 600 cities suffer from water shortages. This already presents an obstacle to the country's economic growth. At the same time, water pollution is becoming increasingly severe. It has become a headache for China's politicians to decide how to allocate, use and manage scarce water resources through economic mechanisms.

Managing Water Scarcity

Unfortunately, China's water law does not provide a clear basis for the right to own and use water. This inevitably has led to battles between different interests—and resulted in water being wasted.

Chongqing, where Tongliang is located, is China's largest municipality under direct central government control. It has suffered from the lack of a system for managing water rights. In the summer of 2006 the city saw a severe drought, with water levels in the Jialing River dropping daily, said Zhou Yi, a researcher with the municipal water authorities. But according to meteorologists there was plenty of rainfall upstream and the river should have been in full flow. In fact, more than 50 hydroelectric plants upstream in western China's Sichuan province were stopping the flow of water, leaving the city dry. The Ministry of Water Resources eventually had to intervene before Sichuan released more water. Three days later after they intervened, the water levels in Chongqing had risen significantly.

Since 1990, one-fifth of Chinese arable land has suffered from drought.

Tongliang is one of Chongqing's most water-poor counties. In August 2006, 260,000 people in the county were short of drinking water; 71,000 had to rely on water shipped in from elsewhere. The land is parched, with cracks wide enough to put your arm in. Even the bamboo, which is normally resistant to drought, has withered.

Although the problems in 2006 were eased by the release of additional water upstream, there are still disputes between Chongqing and Sichuan province over water. Consequently, quick responses to emergency situations are impossible. This has spurred Tongliang to take the lead and implement Chongqing's first regulations on water rights trading.

In March 2007, the water authorities set up a working group to draft new regulations, but it was no easy process.

First, there were differing opinions as to what "water rights" really meant. Former Minister of Water Resources Wang Shucheng once said the way to understand water rights was simply the right to own and use water. But Cui Jianyuan, a professor at Tsinghua University's School of Law, said that water rights refer to the legal acquisition of the right to use or benefit from surface and ground water. There has been a failure to define "water rights" in Chinese legislation.

Second, legal experts said that China's water law has not clarified the situation. If Tongliang's regulations had explicitly defined water rights, they would conflict with existing legislation, so the second article of its rules simply said, "water rights in this document refer to the legal acquisition of the right to use water resources, including the right to water resources development, water abstraction, water usage and drainage."

The original draft of the regulations included the phrase, "upon approval of the municipal water authorities", which has now been changed to just require that the authorities are consulted.

Behind this change lies a typical problem. "Saying 'upon approval' would get into issues of administrative licensing, which is troublesome," said the water management official Liu Shangwu.

Despite its twists and turns, the regulations finally came into effect in January 2008. And although they are by no means perfect, they set an example for water rights reform in China and the use of economic mechanisms to resolve disputes between the water users. Under the scheme, the county water authorities allocate water usage and discharge rights to industries, businesses, villages and towns. What recipients do not use, they can sell.

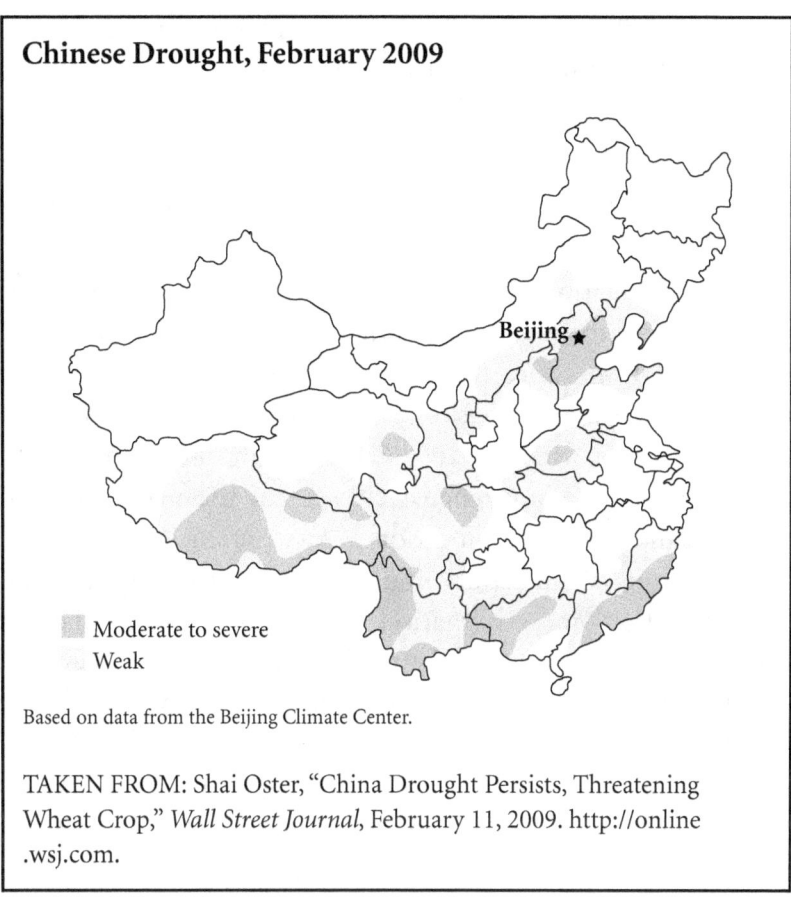

TAKEN FROM: Shai Oster, "China Drought Persists, Threatening Wheat Crop," *Wall Street Journal*, February 11, 2009. http://online.wsj.com.

Tongliang Leads the Way

The system means that the careless use or discharge of water beyond what permits allow will require expensive purchases on the open market—or heavy fines if those purchases are not made. Businesses that use water carefully can reduce their running costs and earn an income by selling off water permits they do not use.

Cao Mingde, a professor at the Southwest University of Politics and Law in Chongqing, said, "Theorists have been exploring ways to reform water rights. But to date, I haven't seen any other regulatory documents. The new regulations in

Tongliang will undoubtedly be a useful trial for regulations covering the entire Chongqing municipality."

When the results are seen from Tongliang, said Lu Feng, a spokesperson for Chongqing's water authorities, then its lessons will be studied nationwide. China is in dire need for standardised practices in water management.

Local regulations have also promoted policy reform at the central government level. Experiences of private trading and local regulations were formally put into practice in interim measures for water allocation, issued by the Ministry of Water Resources on February 1, 2008. The interim document had 17 measures, which comprehensively set out the principles and mechanisms for water allocation across provincial and lower-level groupings. The deputy minister for water resources, Zhou Ying, said that "in combination with the existing regulations on management of water abstraction licenses," the document "forms the start of China's water rights trading system." These interim measures may stimulate a water rights trading market in China, said the *Shanghai Securities News*. Water rights will be sold between different regions, with market mechanisms allocating water in a more beneficial fashion and water saving becoming a reality.

But will such a market be enough to solve China's water crisis? Many experts think it won't be so simple.

China is in dire need for standardised practices in water management.

Pollution trading [where rights to pollute are traded and limited] is an excellent way to use market behaviour for the public good, say economists. But to achieve good results, you need not only the legislation and technology, but also the government acting as a trusted guardian. Otherwise, the results will be unpredictable.

For example, there are vexing questions of how systems can allocate priorities and setting amounts of water that can be drawn or released. How can we ensure equitable distribution? How can we ensure sustainable development? These are tests faced by every level of government.

Li Bairang, who heads a magnetic materials plant—one of Tongliang's major water users, supported the changes. But he also had worries. "If too much water is allocated, there will be no meaningful trade in water rights," Li said. "But if too little is allocated, then high prices for water will be a burden for businesses and stunt local economic development."

The most problematic issue is the lack of any precedent for allocating water rights, admitted Yin Yuanming, an official from the Tongliang water bureau. In the case of a paper plant, for instance, there is a national standard for the amount of water necessary to produce a tonne of paper. But calculating how much wastewater can be released and taking into account the use, recycling and loss of water leaves officials scratching their heads.

And since these limits will impact on profits, there is sure to be resistance to implementation of the new system. Liu Shangwu said he found some teahouses will report the use of 0.16 litres of water per square metre, when they actually use around 20.

The water bureau has put together a number of research groups to develop the regulations and set water use indices for industries, businesses and geographic areas, but it is a huge and complex process.

"It's difficult setting standards," sighs Liu. "There is a long and difficult road ahead."

VIEWPOINT 4

Chile's System of Trading Water Rights Has Hurt Citizens and the Environment

Benjamin Witte

Benjamin Witte is a journalist in Santiago, Chile. In the following viewpoint, he reports that Chile has long had a privatized water market in which water rights can be bought and sold. Critics argue that this system privileges the powerful at the expense of ordinary people. Recently, he reports, there has grown a movement to attempt to nationalize Chile's water. However, he concludes, nationalizing water in Chile faces significant political hurdles, and it is difficult to see how it could be accomplished practically.

As you read, consider the following questions:

1. According to Witte, why are Chile's water wars likely to intensify?
2. Who does Carl Bauer say are the ones who benefit from the current water rights system in Chile?
3. According to Juan Pablo Orrego, what are the political barriers to nationalizing water rights in Chile?

As climate change, pollution, and industrial consumption place increasing pressure on Chile's freshwater supply, a growing chorus of voices is beginning to demand serious re-

Benjamin Witte, "Chile: Movement to Nationalize Water Gains Ground," benwitte .wordpress.com, January 31, 2010. Copyright © 2010 benwitte.wordpress.com. Reproduced by permission of the author.

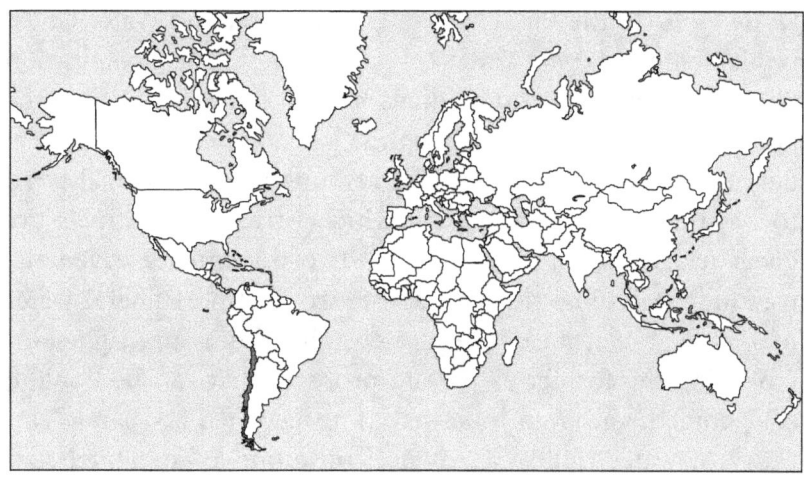

form to the country's privatized water system, first instituted during the dictatorship of Gen. Augusto Pinochet (1973–1990).

Favoring Corporations

Critics point to numerous water-based conflicts to argue that the current system of privately owned usage rights favors the interests of large corporations—particularly mining and energy companies—over the needs of regular citizens. Evidence that Chile's many glaciers are rapidly receding suggests that, in the years to come, the country's "water wars" are only likely to intensify.

In Chile's mineral-rich desert north, mining companies are sucking up what little water exists and leaving rural communities like Quillagua in Region II [in northern Chile] quite literally high and dry. In the central and southern parts of the country, note observers, the system has allowed monopoly-level concentrations of water rights in the hands of just a few energy companies, a situation, they say, that leaves both consumers and the environment at risk.

The origins of the problem, say groups like the recently formed Frente Amplio para la Nacionalizacíon del Agua

(FANA), lie in the Pinochet-era Constitution and Water Code, implemented in 1980 and 1981, respectively. The Constitution says, "The rights that individuals have over water ... gives the holders ownership [of those rights]." The Water Code, in turn, defines the country's freshwater resources as "a national good to be used publicly and over which private individuals are given usage rights." Together the two documents paved the way for what some describe as the world's most liberal water market. The Water Code separated water from land rights, establishing the former as private property that can be bought, sold, traded, and even inherited. It also created a separate category of water rights called "nonconsumptive," designed specifically to promote investment in hydroelectricity production. "It's an especially pure, extreme expression of one theoretical approach to water problems, which is to use market forces," said Carl Bauer, a University of Arizona professor and expert on the Chilean water system. Through the years the system has attracted an influential fan base. In the early 1990s, explained Bauer, the World Bank actively promoted it as a "textbook case of the right way to do things," a model of efficiency that has been particularly successful at attracting private investment.

> Critics ... argue that the current system of privately owned usage rights favors the interests of large corporations ... over the needs of regular citizens.

But by relegating the government's Dirección General de Aguas (DGA) to a purely administrative role, the Water Code undermined the state's ability to properly regulate and thus resolve issues related to competition and environmental degradation, according to Bauer.

"The people who benefit are basically the ones who are rich and powerful enough to get things their way regardless of what the law says," he said. "And as far as the public interest—

both issues of environmental sustainability and social equity and fairness—it isn't well-handled."

Calls for State Control of Water

FANA, launched last September [2008] by a coalition of left-leaning politicians, church leaders, environmentalists, and indigenous groups, insists the only way to address those major shortcomings is by reasserting state control of the resource.

Under the campaign slogan "Recuperemos el Agua para Chile" (Let's Get Chile's Water Back), the Frente is pushing for a constitutional reform that would codify the state's "absolute, exclusive, inalienable, and permanent control of all the nation's continental waters," thus giving the government authority to expropriate water rights as it sees fit.

"The idea is to change what Pinochet did, which was to privatize water rights, and reestablish what already exists in the rest of the world, where water is a national good for public use, where it's not private but instead belongs to society as a whole," Guido Girardi, one of four senators involved in the FANA campaign, told LADB [Latin America Data Base].

> *FANA ... insists the only way to address those major shortcomings is by reasserting state control of the resource.*

FANA's renationalization movement appears to be gaining ground. In late April [2009], the group convened in Santiago for a seminar attended by, among others, former French first lady Danielle Mitterrand, an international advocate for public access to water.

"Water cannot be a source of wealth for certain people or certain private sectors. Water belongs to everyone. It's a common good for all humanity. Everyone should have the right to access this resource," she said.

The issue has also been present in this year's presidential contest. Candidate Alejandro Navarro, a senator from the nascent Movimiento Amplio Social (MAS), has made water nationalization a central part of his platform, as did more-mainstream candidate José Antonio Gomez, president of the Partido Radical (PR). Navarro's momentum is waning, and Gomez recently dropped out of the race. But a third FANA supporter, 35-year-old Partido Socialista (PS) Deputy Marco Enríquez-Ominami, vows to continue campaigning even though his party has already endorsed another candidate, former president Eduardo Frei Ruiz-Tagle (1994–2000). A recent poll suggests that support for the controversial but charismatic Enríquez-Ominami is surging and now stands at approximately 14%.

Political Barriers

While FANA's message is certainly appealing, particularly for members of the Chilean left, the call for renationalization of the country's freshwater has been met with a healthy dose of skepticism, not only from right-wing politicians but also from people who are admittedly "sympathetic" to the concept.

"It's good that the issue is being addressed. And it legitimizes the work of those of us who've raised the subject before. But I'd like to see a more serious effort made in how they actually propose it be done," said veteran environmental activist Juan Pablo Orrego, head of Ecosistemas, a Santiago-based nongovernmental organization (NGO).

> *"It's so clear that water rights are constitutionally protected, that the only way to renationalize water would be, at an absolutely prohibitive cost, to compensate the people whose property rights would be taken or reduced."*

The task is admittedly easier said than done, explained Orrego, who insists there is little willingness within either of

Chile's two dominant political coalitions—the center-left Concertación and right-wing Alianza—to expropriate water rights from the corporate giants that drive Chile's economy.

Carl Bauer, though critical of the current system, agrees. "I understand and I have some sympathy for the reasons behind the argument, the notion that the water law went too far in the privatizing direction. I agree with that. But the proposal to renationalize seems completely impossible to do," he said.

"It's so clear that water rights are constitutionally protected, that the only way to renationalize water would be, at an absolutely prohibitive cost, to compensate the people whose property rights would be taken or reduced," Bauer added. "It would be impossible to pay that amount. The Chilean government doesn't have that money, or wouldn't make it available."

VIEWPOINT 5

Israel Steals Palestinian Water, Resulting in a Water Crisis

Sawsan Ramahi

Sawsan Ramahi is a journalist whose writing has appeared in Middle East Monitor. *In the following viewpoint, Ramahi argues that Israel exercises control over most of the water resources of the Palestinian territory. Ramahi says that Israel diverts these resources for its own use, creating painful water shortages in the territories. Ramahi concludes that the Palestinian territories will never have true sovereignty, and there will never be true peace, unless Israel agrees to allow the territories to control their own water.*

As you read, consider the following questions:

1. According to Ramahi, what means does Israel use to control the waters of the Nile?
2. The Palestinian Water Authority states that what percentage of groundwater used for domestic purposes is not fit for human consumption?
3. How does the separation wall affect Palestinian water, according to Ramahi?

Since 1948 [when Israel was founded] the Israeli authorities have sought to control the majority of the water resources in Palestine.

Sawsan Ramahi, "Israel Is Stealing Palestinian and Arab Water," *Middle East Monitor* March 22, 2010. middleeastmonitor.org.uk. Copyright © 2010 by *Middle East Monitor*. Reproduced by permission.

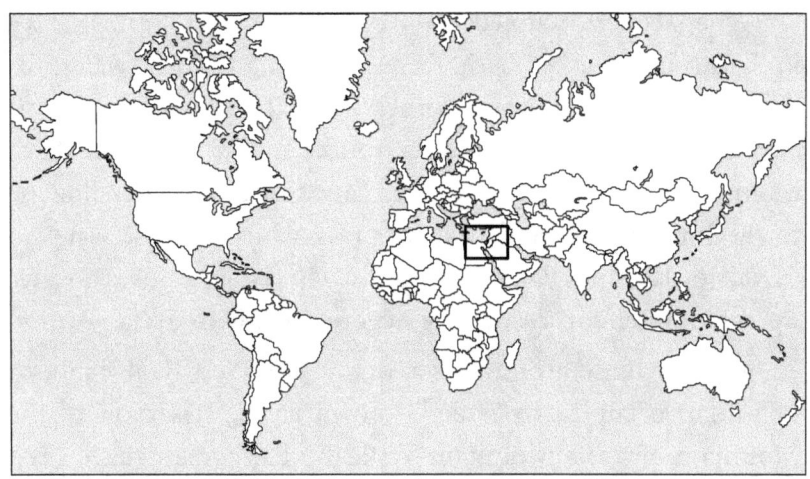

Israel: Water Control

After the 1967 war [in which Israel defeated Egypt, Jordan, and Syria] Israel gained control of the main Arab water sources in the Middle East.

1. The upper Jordan River basin, which originates from Lebanon and Syria:

Israel seized the Jordan River and stored its water in Lake Tiberias (the Sea of Galilee), then transported the water from north to south to feed the different areas of Israel. Israel gets 60% of this water, while Jordan gets 25% and Syria 15%, despite its source being within Syria's borders. It has also prevented the Palestinians from reaching the Jordan River, destroyed all their pumps on the river and evicted the farmers.

When Israel occupied the Golan Heights, it prevented Syria from benefiting from its water; today 30% of Israel's water comes from the Golan Heights.

2. As a result of the diversion of water from the river by Israel the land on both banks has been affected, while the salt level in the water has increased considerably.

3. Yarmouk River basin shared between Jordan and Syria:

Water

When Israel occupied the Golan Heights [a strategic area in Syria], it prevented Syria from benefiting from its water; today 30% of Israel's water comes from the Golan Heights. It also captured the Syrian water source in the Yarmouk River basin. The Golan Heights is the main source of water flowing to the Jordan River and Lake Tiberias, which provide water to Syria, Jordan and Palestine; this is why Israel refuses to give up these water sources in any negotiations with Syria.

4. Large underground reservoirs in the West Bank [an area of Jordan occupied by Israel], known as the Reservoir of the Mountain and the Mountain-Well; the Palestinians have been unable to have access to them since 1967.

- When Israel invaded Lebanon in 1978 it controlled nearly 30% of the Litani River, and during the occupation of Lebanon in 1982 the Israelis benefited from the Wazzani and the Litani's waters, transferring water from them to Israel, while expelling the Lebanese farmers dependent on them.

- In 1989 the Israelis took advantage of the Hasbani and Wazzani waters by installing pipes for themselves, and despite withdrawing from Lebanon in 2000 there are still many Israeli artesian wells on the borders which reduce the groundwater in Lebanese territory.

- Israel uses various means to control the waters of the River Nile, which is 6825 km [kilometres] long and has two main sources; the Equatorial Lakes region of Southern Sudan and the Ethiopian plateau. Israel tries from time to time to cooperate with Ethiopia to build dams and other facilities to control the Nile waters, seeking to reduce Egypt's share of water and put pressure on it in order to secure its share of Nile water. This much has been disclosed by senior officials.

A Water Crisis in the West Bank and Gaza

Since Israel began its occupation of the West Bank and Gaza Strip [part of the Palestinian territory bordering Egypt] it has striven to remain in control of the water resources and diverted water from the Palestinian territories to the cities and settlements set up on the ruins of Palestinian towns destroyed in 1948.

Abdel Rahman Tamimi, a water expert, says that the water battle with the occupation started early on, with military orders and systematic control of water basins, wells and springs since the occupation of the West Bank started in 1967. According to Mr. Tamimi, the water sources were placed under the control of the Israeli Civil Administration in the 1970s, and even after the Oslo agreement [an agreement between Israel and the Palestinians] they remained under Israeli control, *"which exacerbated the water problem in the West Bank."*

The Gaza Strip depends on the coastal underground water reservoir that lies under the Mediterranean Sea between Rafah in the south and north of Mount Carmel, a total area of 2200 km2, of which 400 km2 is located underneath the Gaza Strip. This groundwater is largely independent of the groundwater inside Israel because of the flow of water in an east-west direction into the reservoir; thus, the amount of water available to Palestinians in the Gaza Strip would be reasonable had Israel not confiscated more than 80% of the Palestinian groundwater to make up 20% of the Israelis' total water consumption which stands at 2 billion cubic metres per annum. Due to this, it is estimated that this underground freshwater source will run dry within the next 8 years.

The Palestinian Water Authority has explained that the Gaza Strip is suffering from an annual water deficit of up [to] 70 million cubic metres, noting that as a result of natural population growth in the Strip there are now more than a million and a half people depending on a single source of wa-

Water

ter, the coastal aquifer, to meet their needs. The authority also noted the negative effect on the quality of groundwater due to sea water intrusion, causing high salinity and adding to the high concentration of nitrates in the water, caused by the leakage of sewage and the return underground of irrigation water.

The authority's report states that 90–95% of groundwater used for domestic purposes is not fit for human consumption and not compliant with the World Health Organization standards for drinking water, in terms of quality and quantity, which constitutes a serious threat to health and is a cause of many diseases affecting the population of the Gaza Strip.

It is clear that the Israelis use and waste more water than anyone else in the region.

The water authority says that the rate of water available per person per day is about 80 litres, equivalent to half the recommendation of the World Health Organization.

The West Bank depends on artesian wells for drinking and agricultural purposes. The capacity of running water and water springs in the West Bank ranges, according to the estimates of many experts, between 30 and 50 million cubic metres annually. The springs in the West Bank are estimated to have a capacity of about 75–115 million cubic metres. This was before the Israelis began to use 730 wells in the West Bank for different purposes. There are now 214 wells, of which only 20 are reserved for household purposes, functioning with a production capacity set by the Israeli authorities at about 37.9 million cubic metres annually. The remaining wells have dried up due to pumping from deep wells dug by the Israeli military authorities, or due to being abandoned.

The rate of water consumption of Israeli citizens is 344 million cubic metres per year, while the consumption of Palestinians stands at 93 million cubic metres per year. The domestic consumption of Israelis amounts to 98 million cubic metres, while for Palestinians it comes to 56 million cubic metres per year. It is clear that the Israelis use and waste more water than anyone else in the region.

A study has been made of this issue by the Palestine Economic Policy Research Institute (MAS), prepared by Anan Jayyousi, a lecturer at the Faculty of Engineering in An-Najah [National] University and an expert on the subject of water, and Fathi Srougi, an expert on geopolitical issues relating to water.

Palestinians get just 15% of their own water while the rest is consumed by Israelis.

The Occupation Is the Problem

Jayyousi referred to the volume of water resources in historic Palestine, which is estimated by Israeli hydrologists at about 2250 million cubic metres of renewable water, and includes 3 reserves within the West Bank area producing about 679 million cubic metres of water. According to international law, this water belongs to the Palestinians but they only get 118 million cubic metres. In other words, Palestinians get just 15% of their own water while the rest is consumed by Israelis.

Regarding the use of water for domestic purposes Jayyousi said, "*The supply quantity is estimated at about 130 million cubic metres in the West Bank and Gaza Strip; this means that the average person's water supply is estimated at around 97 litres per day. That said however, the actual average consumption falls short of 70 litres per day, due to the high rate of wasted water.*" This is due to overdue maintenance work on the pipe network, among other reasons. Jayyousi estimates use by the industrial sector at a total of about 9 million cubic metres annually.

Water

In the agricultural sector, the study shows that the average share of irrigated land for an individual is only 0.071 dunams (1000 m2). Furthermore the use of water for irrigation does not exceed 45 cubic metres per person, which is less than the prevailing rates in Jordan and Israel.

It must be noted that Israel has not allowed the Palestinians to control their water according to their needs, but tied them up in resolutions through which the Jewish state:

1. Limits the amount of water withdrawals to no more than 100 cubic metres per hour.
2. Limits the depth of drilled wells to 140 metres, requiring specific types of old pumps which are permitted in the West Bank, essentially limiting the capacity to extract water from these wells.
3. Dug huge wells in strategic areas where water accumulates across the West Bank and the Gaza Strip in order to steal Palestinian water (60 wells in the West Bank, 43 in the Gaza Strip, and 26 along the armistice line between Gaza and Israel).
4. Adopted a strategy of building small dams to prevent the natural flow of surface water to the Palestinian areas thus allowing the transfer of high-quality water from Israeli settlements in the Palestinian territories into Israeli cities, or selling this water to the Palestinians.
5. Builds settlements such that they are in areas with the highest quality underground water reserves to allow Israel to seize the water, directly or indirectly, a policy which has lead to the depletion of groundwater in the Gaza Strip.

According to a study by the Palestinian Information Centre, 150 Palestinian residential communities in the West Bank are not part of the water distribution networks. Most residents in these communities suffer from water shortages.

Forcing Palestinians to Leave

Resolution of Palestine's water problems is utterly dependent on cooperation from Israel; and inaction will lead to a serious environmental disaster in Gaza and to continued suffering for many water-starved communities in the West Bank. Water shortage also undermines the agricultural sector and prevents it from developing, with consequences for the food security and economic well-being of the Palestinian population. . . .

What can be perceived here is that many of Israel's leaders, while appearing to make concessions to the Palestinians, . . . have concentrated their policy towards creating 'facts on the ground' that will make life for the Palestinians impossible, hence creating the 'positive conditions' required to induce people to leave.

Alice Gray, "The Water Crisis in Gaza,"
International Viewpoint Online, February 2007.
www.internationalviewpoint.org.

Hebron's Water Problem

The city of Hebron, in the south of the West Bank, is considered the most deprived Palestinian city in terms of lack of water, where the average Palestinian individual consumes as little as 10 litres of water per day for extended periods of time.

The water problem in Hebron is primarily a result of the Israeli occupation authority's control over water basins; Palestinians are not permitted to dig wells and the Israelis do not provide the water necessary for daily use. An example illustrates the measures to which the Israelis are prepared to go with this: The Israeli army surprised four citizens from the village of Soba, west of Hebron as they were drilling a well to collect rainwater; they were surrounded and arrested, their equipment was confiscated; they were fined and finally released with strict orders not to resume drilling.

Abdel-Rahman Rajoub has commented on this: "*What is strange is that one of the detainees said that they had told the investigating officer, during the eight days that they were in custody, that the drilling was simply for the purpose of collecting rainwater. The officer accused them of 'stealing groundwater' and told them that rainwater collection is 'forbidden'.*"

The water problem in Hebron is primarily a result of the Israeli occupation authority's control over water basins.

To the east of Hebron, the Israeli army destroyed four large pools that collect water, and deprived large areas of agricultural land of irrigation water, causing great losses to dozens of farmers. Several said that this is in order "*to harass the Palestinians and force them into leaving the area, in order to clear it for settlement building.*"

The residents in this fertile region have resorted to making holes in water pipes to get the water needed to irrigate their crops, even though this is at the expense of their drinking water.

The Separation Wall

In addition to the tactics noted above that are employed by the Israelis to seize Palestinian water, the occupation authority has used the illegal "*separation wall*" [a barrier constructed by Israel to separate Israel and the West Bank] to ensure that it also has control of three of the most important Palestinian water basins, depriving the Palestinians of their right of access in order to send this water to settlements. As the construction of what is basically an apartheid wall continues in the West Bank, Palestinian official sources confirm that it will annex to

Israel about 95% of the water that is accessible in the western basin, which is estimated at about 362 million metres.

The area isolated behind the western part of the wall lies above two basins; the western basin and northeast basin, which have an estimated annual capacity of 507 million cubic metres. The area isolated in the east lies completely over the eastern basin which has an estimated capacity of 172 million cubic metres annually. Water is extracted from these aquifers by pumping from wells or from the natural springs. The estimated number of groundwater wells in these regions is 165 with a pumping capacity of 33 million cubic metres per year; the number of springs is estimated to be 53, with a capacity of 22 million cubic metres per year.

In the Jenin, Qalqilyah and Tulkarem provinces, the land annexed by the wall is entirely congruent with the locations of groundwater, meaning that all the groundwater reserves are on the wrong, that is the Israeli, side of the wall. This renders as useless any Palestinian attempt to extract water from those reserves; as such, the wall threatens to drive to extinction irrigated agriculture in the north of the West Bank.

Israel drains the Palestinian groundwater, which has led to an increase in the levels of salts, nitrates and chlorides, as well as heavy metal contaminations such as copper and lead.

According to the report by the Palestinian Water Authority, the wall has led to the loss of Palestinian access to more than 36 wells, which includes 23 located directly on the route of the wall, and 13 others nearby that were used for agriculture and drinking; these wells now lie between the wall and the old "*Green Line*" (the 1967 armistice line). The wells used to pump about 55 million cubic metres per annum, around 25% of the total extracted from the Western reservoir. The occupation authorities are also seeking, through the route of the wall, to seize more than 400 m3 which constitutes the entire capacity of the renewable groundwater west basin, of which most is accumulated within the borders of the Palestinian West Bank.

Israel drains the Palestinian groundwater, which has led to an increase in the levels of salts, nitrates and chlorides, as well as heavy metal contaminations such as copper and lead, which deem it unsuitable for drinking or agricultural use. The draining of wells has also caused severe leakage of salty groundwater into fresh groundwater in the West Bank; in the Gaza Strip seawater has leaked into the groundwater basin to fill the vacuum.

The Palestinian Ministry of Health confirms the results of tests showing that the water in the networks is contaminated frequently, leading to the spread of diseases among the population. Analysis has shown a link between the contamination of water and the spread of diseases, such as typhoid fever, meningitis and cholera. An official in the Ministry of Health monitoring committee confirmed that they are examining all water continually, whether it is drinking water, for agriculture or for other uses. He said, *"There is an ongoing process of filtration and purification of the water in the wells which reduces the contamination and salt levels in the water."* The Israeli security forces hinder or prevent the implementation of many projects that have the potential to solve this problem, he added.

No Peace Without Water

From the above we note that Israel is the cause of the water crisis for Palestinians in particular and for Arabs in general, a fact that the Jewish state refuses to acknowledge. Israel will continue with its plans to control more water resources, especially as it seeks to attract ever-greater numbers of Jewish immigrants.

Unfortunately, the Oslo agreement deferred negotiations of the issue of water to the anticipated "final status" agreement, which was one mistake amongst many committed by the Palestinian negotiators. By agreeing to defer consideration of the most important issues until the "final status" talks (including the status of Jerusalem, the return of refugees as well as the water issue), they have allowed Israel to introduce many changes and "*facts on the ground*" which the Palestinians will just have to accept.

It is worth remembering that unless proposals include Palestinian control over their own natural water resources, it is useless to talk about an independent Palestinian state, with real sovereignty over its air, land and sea.

The Jewish state avoids discussing the core issues such as the water problems of the Palestinians and tries to shift the focus to long-term solutions such as the search for alternative water sources, desalination plants and a reduction in the amount needed for agriculture.

It is worth remembering that unless proposals include Palestinian control over their own natural water resources, it is useless to talk about an independent Palestinian state, with real sovereignty over its air, land and sea. It is equally useless, to consider achieving genuine peace.

The United Nations should take its responsibilities seriously and oblige Israel to end its illegal occupation of Palestinian land, giving back to the Palestinians their inalienable rights, including control of its natural resources. As long as Israel is treated with kid gloves by the international community, as a state which is above the law, peace talks—proximity or direct—will continue to be diplomatic devices to give the Israelis more time to create more facts on the ground; and genuine peace and justice will remain as elusive as ever.

VIEWPOINT 6

The Middle East Water Crisis Is the Result of the Failures of Many Regional Governments

Gidon Bromberg

Gidon Bromberg is the Israeli director of Friends of the Earth Middle East. In the following viewpoint, he says that the water shortage in the Middle East may result in the drying up of the Jordan River. He argues that the water crisis is the result of poor management by and conflict between countries including Jordan, Syria, and Israel. Bromberg notes that Friends of the Earth Middle East has enlisted local communities to focus on and advocate for water conservation. He suggests that communication between these communities could lead to peace and to pressure for better conservation policies by national governments.

As you read, consider the following questions:

1. What saved much of the lower Jordan from becoming a desiccated channel, according to Bromberg?
2. What does Bromberg say is the underlying reason that many great rivers have started to run dry?
3. What is the Red-Dead project, and why does Bromberg oppose it?

Gidon Bromberg, "Will the Jordan River Keep on Flowing?" *Yale Environment 360*, September 18, 2008. Copyright © 2008 Gidon Bromberg. Reproduced by permission of the author.

Managing Water Scarcity

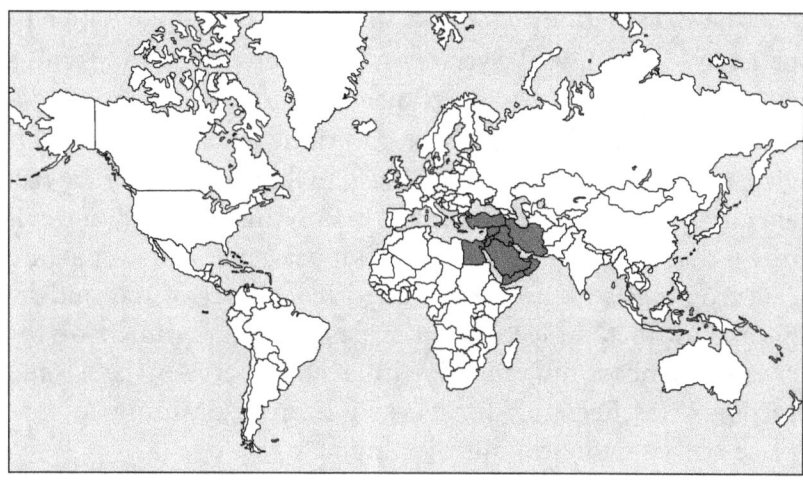

The River Jordan has flowed freely for thousands of years, its name immortalized in the Hebrew Bible and its lush upper reaches once known as the gates to the Garden of Eden. This summer [2008], however, large sections of this storied river were reduced to a trickle, the water so low that grass fires spread freely across the Jordan Valley between Israel and Jordan. Steadily drained over the past half century to quench the thirst and grow the crops of the people of Israel, Jordan, Syria, and the Palestinian territories, the Jordan River has been dealt a deathblow recently by a severe drought and by yet another tributary dam, this one on the Jordanian-Syrian border.

The Disappearing Jordan

In recent years, all that saved much of the lower Jordan from becoming a desiccated channel has been the agricultural runoff, raw human sewage, diverted saline spring water, and contaminated wastes from fish farms that have been pumped into it. But now even that effluent barely restores a flow to the Jordan, the river where Jesus Christ was baptized and which has long been a vital stopover on the migratory pathway of tens of millions of birds en route between Europe and Africa.

107

The degradation highlights the failure of the governments of Israel, Jordan, and Syria to take serious steps to rescue a 205-mile river that has deep meaning for Christianity, Judaism, and Islam. Although these governments have paid lip service to bringing the Jordan back to life, they have in fact encouraged water withdrawals—mainly for irrigated agriculture—that have led to its near-disappearance. This ecological catastrophe has been overshadowed by decades of war and regional conflict. Indeed, for the past 60 years, much of the river—a fenced and mined border zone between Israel and Jordan—has been off-limits, enabling its draining to take place out of sight and out of mind.

The governments of the region have blamed the conflict for their lack of action, but as the citizens' group I help run—EcoPeace/Friends of the Earth Middle East—has shown, international cooperation to resuscitate the Jordan is possible. Working with local communities, my Jordanian, Palestinian, and Israeli colleagues are striving to restore water to the river. The goal of our group—the region's only multinational organization—is to become a catalyst for comprehensive water policy reform. We are aided by an unexpected phenomenon: In a region where people often feel helpless after years of turmoil, our efforts at environmental peacemaking offer an opportunity for constructive action, dialogue, and cooperation.

Rivers as Tools

The story of the depletion of the Jordan is hardly unique. Around the world, human activity has pulled so much water out of great rivers—the Indus on the Indian subcontinent, the Yellow in China, the Rio Grande along the U.S.-Mexico border—that they now either disappear before reaching the sea or contain long sections that seasonally run dry. The underlying reason is always the same: We view rivers not as valuable in themselves, supplying vital "ecosystem services" to people, fish, animals, and plants, but rather as merely tools for humans and economic development.

That was certainly the case in the early days of the formation of Israel, when the dream of nation building was to "make the desert bloom." In the 1950s, that dream was married to advanced engineering as Israel's National Water Carrier diverted about a third of the original flow of the Jordan to Tel Aviv and the farms of the Negev desert. Subsequent Israeli water withdrawals, coupled with scores of dam and canal projects on tributaries in Syria and Jordan, claimed the rest of the river's water. For ages, the Sea of Galilee has fed the longest stretch of the river, the lower Jordan, but today not a drop of freshwater flows out of the sea into the river. The largest tributary to the lower Jordan, the Yarmouk River, has similarly had all its waters diverted by Syria and Jordan. As these insults to the Jordan have accumulated, water disputes in this rain-starved region have grown ever more contentious, with unequal water allocations—coupled with violence and occupation—becoming a powerful human rights issue and an additional source of animosity.

Around the world, human activity has pulled so much water out of great rivers . . . that they now either disappear before reaching the sea or contain long sections that seasonally run dry.

Just as the Jordan is hitting bottom, another troubling development is unfolding. The World Bank has selected two consulting firms to study the feasibility of pumping water from the Red Sea to the Dead Sea, the terminus of the Jordan River, via a massive and staggeringly expensive pipeline. Because of the Jordan's catastrophic reduction in flows—from a historic level of 1.3 billion cubic meters annually to only about 70,000 cubic meters now—the surface area of the Dead Sea has shrunk by a third in the past 50 years and the level of the sea, the world's lowest point, is dropping by a meter a year. Rather than tackling the root problem destroying the river and draining the Dead Sea—which would require restoring flows to the Jordan—the World Bank, supported by Jordan, Israel, and the Palestinian Authority, is throwing its weight behind a huge public works project that could easily cost $5 billion to $10 billion and will likely have damaging ecological consequences.

The so-called Red-Dead project would be rendered obsolete if nations bordering the Jordan would begin putting water back into the river. But with regional governments taking little action, Friends of the Earth Middle East has stepped in to push for measures that will gradually return water to the Jordan. Our approach is two-pronged: The first is a program called Good Water Neighbors, in which we work with nine river communities—four Jordanian, three Israeli, and two Palestinian, all located on opposite banks—to conserve water and educate people about the value of the Jordan and its wetlands. The second, and more challenging, task is to persuade national leaders to make the tough choices that will revitalize the Jordan: charging more for water, removing large subsidies to agricultural water users, and adopting large-scale conservation programs.

Water and Peace

Our group has made progress because we are a grassroots, multinational effort with Jordanian, Israeli and Palestinian staff members working inside their own communities while simultaneously reaching out to nationalities across the river. One of our core beliefs is that the region will never achieve a lasting peace until we begin talking directly to each other. Tackling a crucial environmental challenge that affects us all is a good start.

In each community, a staff person from Friends of the Earth Middle East, who is a local resident, has pushed an ambitious agenda with adults and youth. The teams have begun water conservation and rainwater harvesting programs in schools and other buildings. They have publicized the plight of the river and have gathered 15,000 signatures on petitions that were presented to elected officials. They have persuaded Israeli, Palestinian, and Jordanian mayors from both banks to sign memoranda of understanding, committing themselves to help bring the river back to life. Recently, members of the different communities have been visiting each other to see their towns and water conservation programs. Last year [2007], officials in Jordan and Israel agreed to create a Peace Park at the confluence of the Jordan and Yarmouk rivers that will include a bird sanctuary, eco-lodges, a visitor's center, and nature and heritage trails. And given the river's importance in religious history, we're enlisting representatives of the Muslim, Christian, and Jewish faiths in the campaign. Rehabilitating the Jordan has become much more than an environmental crusade; it's now an international project backed by schoolchildren, community leaders, and scientists.

One of our core beliefs is that the region will never achieve a lasting peace until we begin talking directly to each other. Tackling a crucial environmental challenge that affects us all is a good start.

These are small steps, but set against the backdrop of widespread hostility—and the absence of similar regional initiatives—our programs take on greater meaning. What is needed now is action from the Israeli and Jordanian governments, hopefully to be joined in the near future by Syria. They could start by creating an international commission to manage the Jordan, similar to the commissions that govern North America's Great Lakes and Europe's Rhine River. Regional governments and international donor states, including the U.S., also need to take a hard look at the proposed Red Sea–Dead Sea canal, a potential boondoggle that could cause major problems, including mixing the marine water of the Red

Sea with the freshwater of the Dead Sea, which could change the composition of the Dead Sea and cause algal blooms. The wiser, and far cheaper, alternative is to revive the Dead Sea by restoring its main source of water—the Jordan River.

For decades now, conflict and human arrogance have been responsible for the demise of the Jordan. Cooperation in search of peace and sustainability is the only hope to restore it to health.

VIEWPOINT 7

Nile River Countries Struggle over Water Rights

Joshua Kyalimpa

Joshua Kyalimpa is an independent radio journalist and producer based in Kampala, Uganda, and the managing director of Opsett Media Ltd. In the following viewpoint, he reports that Lake Victoria, which feeds the Nile, is shrinking. He notes that Egypt, Sudan, Uganda, and other countries that use the Nile are trying to reach an agreement to preserve and utilize its water. If they fail, he concludes, conservation and developmental goals may be unreachable.

As you read, consider the following questions:

1. What is the area and population of the Nile basin, according to the Nile Basin Initiative?
2. According to Kyalimpa, what issues are addressed by article 4, article 5, article 6, and article 8 of the new Nile River treaty he discusses?
3. What clause does Egypt want included in the treaty, and why does Kyalimpa say that other nations are resisting?

Ten years of negotiations over a new protocol governing shared use of the Nile River are hanging in the balance, with Egypt and Sudan refusing to give up their present power

Joshua Kyalimpa, "Nile River Countries Argue over Water Rights," africanagriculture blog.com, January 27, 2009. Copyright © 2009 by Inter Press Service. All rights reserved. Reproduced by permission.

Water

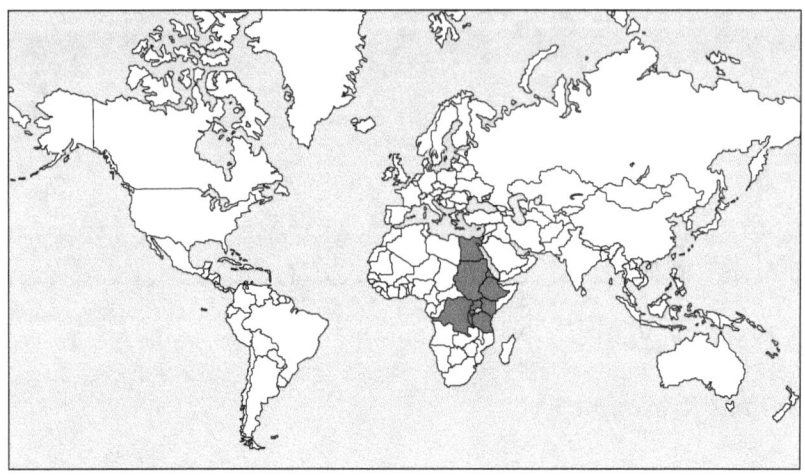

over how much water is used by countries further upstream. The current agreement prohibits countries downstream from using Nile waters beyond an agreed curve, and gives Egypt powers to monitor the flow at key points.

Shrinking Lake Victoria

"The technocrats had worked out all the paperwork for a good protocol but the politicians have thrown a clean piece of cloth in the mud," says Professor [Isaac] Afunaduula, chair of the Nile Basin Discourse Forum, a consortium of civil society organisations looking at issues along the world's longest river.

The article in the new draft which has caused the stalemate is 14b, concerning water security. Water use by countries upstream has long been restricted by the terms of the colonial agreement signed on their behalf by Britain in 1929, and reaffirmed in 1954. The Nile basin has a population of 160 million people in an area of 3.1 million square kilometres—including 81,500 sq km of lakes and 70,000 sq km of swamps, according to statistics from the Nile Basin Initiative, a body set up by Nile riparian states with funding from various donors to harmonise policy over the Nile.

Over the years, water levels in Lake Victoria, a major source of water for the Nile, have been falling. Water levels in 2008, were 2.5 metres lower than three years earlier. This is believed to be due to a combination of factors, including declining rainfall and increased use—and it is causing panic among states that share the Nile.

> *[Lake Victoria] water levels in 2008 were 2.5 metres lower than three years earlier. This ... is causing panic among states that share the Nile.*

The 10 countries sharing the river under the Nile Basin Initiative have been negotiating a new framework agreement to manage the river's water for the last 10 years. The countries are Kenya, Burundi, Rwanda, Tanzania, Eritrea, Ethiopia, Sudan, Egypt, [Democratic Republic of the] Congo and Uganda. The Nile River Basin Cooperative Framework's article 6 talks about protection and conservation of the basin and its ecosystem and environmentalists look at this as a milestone in maintaining the water levels from a wider catchment area feeding into the lake.

The Dangers of Deadlock

But Frank Muramuzi of Uganda's National Association of Professional Environmentalists believes a deadlock could undermine regional conservation and development activities under the Nile Basin Initiative. He thinks a new protocol would guarantee countries like Egypt and Sudan more water. "The protocol would set a framework for sustainable use of water resources from the river Nile," says Muramuzi.

But if the status quo remains, waters from Lake Victoria, the major reservoir for the Nile, will continue to recede and shortages may result into conflicts, he adds. The treaty being considered now also has five other major clauses which generated heated debate in previous negotiations. These include article 4, which is on equitable and reasonable use of the Nile waters, article 5 (prevention of harm to the waters), article 6 (protection and conservation of the basin and its ecosystem) and article 8 (prior informed consent before using the waters). Egypt and Sudan, which have largely desert land, have been opposed to the treaty, fearing it would cut them off from the Nile waters.

A deadlock could undermine regional conservation and development activities under the Nile Basin Initiative.

In the new document, clause 14b concerning prior informed consent was amended after Kenya, Tanzania and the Democratic Republic of the Congo pushed for its alteration to "information concerning planned measures". The new wording puts a check on the 1929 treaty, which required the riparian states to seek permission before using the Nile waters. The document further provides for establishment of a Nile Basin Commission, with its headquarters in Entebbe, Uganda.

The decision on the matter is now in suspense because negotiators have passed the issue on to the 10 heads of state of the Nile basin to conclude. Callist Tindimugaya, Uganda's commissioner in the Ministry of Water, said that what can be done now is to continue cooperating, pending the resolution of the contentious clause in the new protocol.

Upstream Nations vs. Downstream Nations

According to Professor Patrick Rubaihayo, an expert on development based in Makerere University, Kampala, many of the upstream countries risk missing millennium development goal targets should a new and more equitable protocol not be signed. "Continuing extreme poverty is one of the consequences if a new protocol is not signed," he said. A vibrant agriculture sector is seen as an essential vehicle for development,

> ## Control of the Nile
>
> The 4,135-mile-long Nile River flows through ten countries in its long journey from southern Rwanda to its delta on the Mediterranean Sea. The basin has been settled for more than 4,000 years and is considered the cradle of civilization. Over the millennia, empires have risen and fallen, but the Nile has endured as a symbol of the impermanence of human institutions and the durability of natural systems. Since the dawn of history, irrigation along the banks of the Nile has thrived. Together with fishing, farming along the Nile River provides sustenance to 300 million people. In the past, the dominant country controlled the waters of the Nile—typically it was Egypt. Since 1959, Egypt and Sudan have essentially split the total water of the Nile between themselves, ignoring the other countries involved.
>
> Peter Rogers and Susan Leal,
Running Out of Water: The Looming Crisis and
Solutions to Conserve Our Most Precious Resource, 2010.

but Rubaihayo cannot envision this developing without investment in massive irrigation schemes. The colonial agreement on sharing the Nile's waters makes these schemes difficult because Egypt and Sudan must approve irrigation projects, and flatly refuse.

Uganda's Minister for Water, Jennifer Namuyangu, says the discussion is an opportunity for countries like Uganda to correct a historical anomaly. She says Uganda will not accept a lopsided pact over the use of the Nile. Professor Afunaduula believes Egypt's refusal to sign a new protocol could be based on a calculation that one of their own is in line to become head of the Nile Basin Initiative and therefore influence the process. According to the charter that set up the initiative, the head rotates among the member countries of the basin and the director serves a term of two years. The current head is Henrietta Ndombe, a Congolese who will lead the organisation until September 2010 when someone from Egypt will take over.

Egypt and Sudan must approve irrigation projects, and flatly refuse.

Egypt wants a clause which states that other countries sharing the Nile should not use water to the detriment of another country. Other countries want that clause deleted altogether because of the implication that countries upstream will have to get consent to construct hydroelectric dams and irrigation projects.

But according to Gordon Mumbo, who is in charge of confidence building among member states of the Nile basin, there is now thinking that the matter should be passed on to the council of foreign ministers because the heads of state have been hard to get together for a signing. He says the chance to sign at the sidelines of the Africa union summit in Cairo, Egypt, four months ago was missed because of disagreements.

Periodical and Internet Sources Bibliography

The following articles have been selected to supplement the diverse views presented in this chapter.

Al Jazeera	"Egypt Reasserts Nile Water Rights," April 20, 2010. http://english.aljazeera.net.
Alexei Barrionuevo	"Chilean Town Withers in Free Market for Water," *New York Times*, March 14, 2009.
BBC News	"Report: Palestinians Denied Water," October 27, 2009. http://news.bbc.co.uk.
Damian Carrington	"Desertification Is Greatest Threat to Planet, Expert Warns," *Guardian*, December 16, 2010.
Circle of Blue	"Chile Considers Constitutional Reform of Freshwater Rights," January 28, 2010. www.circleofblue.org.
William Davison	"Congo, Burundi Are Set to Sign Nile River Water Accord Rejected by Egypt," Bloomberg.com, January 20, 2011. www.bloomberg.com.
Eden Foundation	"Desertification—A Threat to the Sahel," August 1994. www.eden-foundation.org.
Chris Edwards	"A Desert Hot Spot? The Sahel Is Recognised as the Region Most Prone to Desertification. But There Is Increasing Evidence Suggesting the Process Is Being Reversed in Some Areas," *Geographical*, February 2005.
Fan Fengyu	"China's Worsening Water Crisis," Forbes.com, September 28, 2009. www.forbes.com.
Lydia Polgreen	"In Niger, Trees and Crops Turn Back the Desert," *New York Times*, February 11, 2007.
Ehud Zion Waldoks	"Jordan River to Run Dry by Next Year," *Jerusalem Post*, May 3, 2010.

CHAPTER 3

Access to Safe Water

VIEWPOINT 1

China's Poor Environmental Record Has Poisoned Water Supplies

Andreas Lorenz

Andreas Lorenz is the China correspondent for Spiegel Online. *In the following viewpoint he reports on a chemical plant catastrophe on the Songhua River that poisoned the water in the city of Harbin. Lorenz argues that the disaster highlights the downside of China's economic expansion, which has resulted in endemic environmental degradation. Lorenz also accuses Chinese officials of regularly lying to minimize environmental problems. He argues that water and air pollution and industrial accidents seriously damage the health of the Chinese people, and he concludes that the government has no will to make improvements.*

As you read, consider the following questions:

1. How many people does Lorenz say will potentially be affected by the Songhua River disaster?
2. Who is Pan Yue, and why does he believe that China's economic miracle will come to an end, as reported by the author?
3. How many Chinese people does Lorenz say die prematurely each year because of air pollution, and what is the cost to the gross domestic product?

Andreas Lorenz, "Choking on Chemicals in China," translated by Christopher Sultan, *Spiegel Online International*, November 28, 2005. Copyright © 2005 by New York Times Syndicate. All rights reserved. Reproduced by permission.

Water

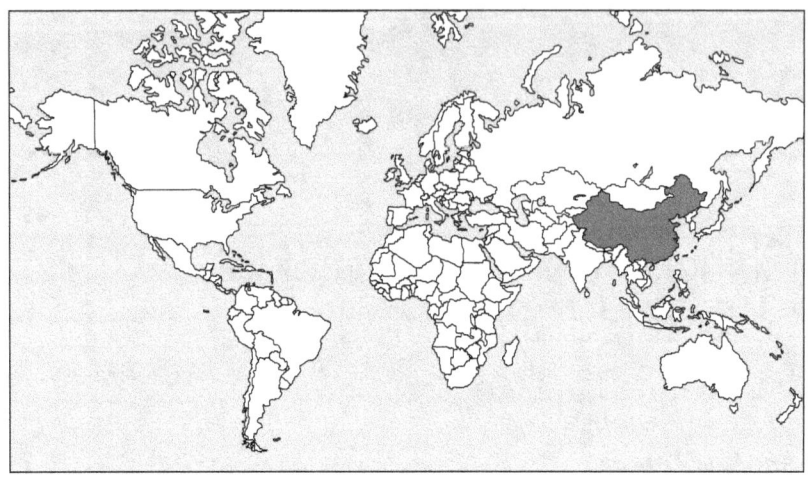

On Friendship Street in the northeast Chinese city of Harbin, hundreds of people carrying white canisters, red buckets, plastic bowls and cooking pots wait for a tanker truck. They have been waiting here in the bitter cold since early morning—though the water delivery isn't scheduled until 11 am. Two police officers and three women from the neighborhood committee keep an eye on the crowd. Their job is to ensure that the water is fairly distributed when it arrives—at about five liters per person.

Other Harbin residents have lined in front of the Century Buddha Restaurant on Yilan Street. Twice a day, for an hour and a half at a time, the owner dispenses free water from his private well. Meanwhile, customers at a local supermarket make off with entire pallets of sparkling water and juice. "We are now frugal with water," says a woman in a red woolen cap. "First we use it to clean vegetables, then to wash our hands and finally to flush the toilet."

The water emergency in Harbin, an industrial city of 3.8 million, comes on the heels of an environmental catastrophe with as yet unforeseeable consequences. About 100 tons of toxic chemicals have been floating down the Songhua River ever since an explosion in Jilin, located 400 kilometers (248 miles) upstream from Harbin, released highly toxic benzene compounds. At least five people were killed and dozens injured in the Nov. 13 accident in Chemical Factory 101, and the slick, slowly traveling downriver toward Russia, threatens the drinking water supply for more than 10 million people between the northeast Chinese city of Harbin and Khabarovsk in Siberia.

True to form, the Chinese Communist Party attempted to twist the disaster into a propaganda victory, sending convoys of water trucks decorated with red banners ("Love the people—deliver water") from other cities and ordering soldiers to drill for new wells. But try as it might, the People's Republic cannot obscure the sheer magnitude of this environmental catastrophe. Never before has a city as large as Harbin had to shut off the taps to avoid poisoning its residents.

Never before has a city as large as Harbin had to shut off the taps to avoid poisoning its residents.

The World's Toxic Waste Dump

Even if water began flowing once again to the city's residents on Tuesday, the horrific environmental catastrophe reveals the flipside of the socialist economic miracle. Secretiveness and sluggish crisis management highlight the price the Chinese are paying for their boom. And even as westerners envy the half-communist, half-capitalist country for its impressive growth figures and endless backyard market, China is no longer merely the world's factory. It is also the world's toxic waste dump.

China's rise as a global power, achieved with high economic growth rates, is reminiscent of the conditions in the era of early capitalism. Everything that drives production is good, and everything that slows it down—safety technology, for example, that prevents industrial accidents from leading to massive factory explosions—is harmful. The result is exploding tanks, burning factories, collapsing mine pits and all manner of toxic leaks. According to official statistics, 350 Chinese die each day in industrial accidents, but the unofficial figure is likely to be much higher. "Occupational safety is a serious problem, because the number of accidents and deaths remains high," said Wang Dexue, Deputy Director of the State Office of Occupational Safety, commenting on the horrifying figures from the country's manufacturing industries.

China is no longer merely the world's factory. It is also the world's toxic waste dump.

Adding to the problems are economic reforms that have made many businessmen greedy. China's laissez-faire brand of socialism doesn't prevent executives from spending their money on cars and villas instead of investing it in worker safety and environmental protection. Although the government is constantly vowing to monitor manufacturers more closely, local officials and party leaders are often in bed with the captains of industry in China. This Mafia-like alliance between the politically and economically ambitious is known as "local protectionism."

Chen Bangzhu, an environmental expert on Beijing's Parliamentary Council, says he recognizes an "irrational development" in his country. In an interview earlier this year, Pan Yue, the deputy minister of government environmental agency SEPA, predicted a bitter end to the economic miracle. "This boom will soon come to an end," he said in an interview with SPIEGEL, "because the environment isn't cooperating anymore."

Swimming or Suicide in the Yangtze

The negative consequences of the boom are devastating. Five of the world's 10 most polluted cities are in China. More than two-thirds of all Chinese rivers and lakes are turning into sewers—even before the recent accident, the Songhua River was hardly a model of cleanliness—and more than 360 million people have no access to clean drinking water. A toxic soup splashes through the country's waterways, while people living along the banks die from cancer at above-average rates. Nowadays, the then 72-year-old former party chairman Mao Zedong's legendary swimming outing in the Yangtze River in 1966 would no longer be seen as evidence of his strength, but more as a suicide attempt.

The Chinese capital itself is suffocating in its own filth and pollution. On many days of the year, Beijing is covered by a dome of pollution made up of the exhaust gases from more than 2 million cars, as well as the dust from construction sites and cement plants. "The government doesn't want to talk about it before the 2008 Olympic Games, but the level of exhaust gases in Beijing's air is dangerously high," warns a high-ranking government official. Satellite measurements have revealed that Beijing is covered by a blanket of nitrogen dioxide of previously unheard-of proportions.

More than two-thirds of all Chinese rivers and lakes are turning into sewers . . . and more than 360 million people have no access to clean drinking water.

And there is no improvement in sight. To meet its rapidly growing demand for energy, the government is building coal power plants, with more than 500 planned for the next few years. Although China has its fair share of windmills and Beijing promotes renewable energies, well over two-thirds of the country's electricity requirements are met by burning coal.

"Because energy is so scarce, the Chinese are now burning anything that looks like coal," complains a German environmental expert. And because filters are not in compliance with international standards, emissions of sulfur and nitrogen oxides are "a dimension higher" than in other industrialized nations. "Half of all coal power plants," admits a SEPA official, "violate environmental regulations."

$250 Billion of Pollution

The People's Republic, which could soon surpass the United States as the world's largest producer of greenhouse gases, has lost its ecological balance and is paying a heavy price as a result. About 400,000 people die prematurely each year because of the polluted air they breathe. Experts estimate the annual loss at 8 to 15 percent of the gross domestic product—or up to $250 billion—a figure that does not include the costs of treating cancer, skin conditions and bronchitis.

The Chinese leadership has become increasingly concerned about the possibility that environmental damage could jeopardize China's industrial ascent. After the Harbin incident, even Prime Minister Wen Jiabao admitted that the environmental situation is "bleak" and called for "sustainable growth." But many other party leaders see this kind of talk as nothing but Western social nonsense. They prefer to follow the lead of Mao, who summed up his take on the environment in 1958 when he said: "Make the high mountain bow its head; make the river yield its way." Today's comrades, profiting handsomely from industrial growth, believe it is cheaper to clean up in the distant future than to invest in protecting the environment today.

Whenever catastrophes do occur, the Communist Party responds using the same old Stalinist approach.

Besides, the system promotes environmental dramas such as the one playing out in Harbin now. The careers of party functionaries are tied to economic success figures, not to fresh air and clean water. "The only thing that counts, when it comes to keeping their jobs or getting a promotion, is what they're doing to increase the gross domestic product," says Sze

Pang-cheung of Greenpeace China in Hong Kong. Chinese courts, says Pang-cheung, are notorious for disallowing environmental suits or failing to execute sentences against polluters. Besides, it is usually cheaper for factories to pay fines than to install filters or treatment systems.

Whenever catastrophes do occur, the Communist Party responds using the same old Stalinist approach. In Harbin, as with the SARS crisis two years ago, authorities initially tried to conceal or at least downplay the true scope of the disaster. At first, the managers of the Jilin Petrochemical Company claimed that the accident posed no danger whatsoever to the Songhua River. State-owned television followed suit and announced that the "accident caused no serious environmental damage." And when the Harbin city administration announced its plans to shut off the water supply, it first offered the transparent excuse that the pipes needed "maintenance work." No one believed that the city's entire system of pipes was shut down for maintenance at -10°C (14°F), and the icy city was soon filled with rumors of terrorist attacks or a predicted earthquake.

Unjustifiable Lies

Anyone with money fled the city by train or air. Those who stayed cleared the shelves in the food sections of places like Wal-Mart and Metro. The Beijing youth newspaper called the PR gaffe "unjustifiable lies."

Bit by bit—and fully ten days after environmental officials had detected the toxic spill—the government began revealing the facts. "They should have told us the truth from the very beginning," complains Zhao, a retiree doing his morning calisthenics in a blue winter coat and blue cap. Once again, he says, the poorest are the worst off. "I must now depend on expensive bottled water. And if I fall ill because of the poisons in the Songhua River, I'll have to pay the medical bills myself."

VIEWPOINT 2

Haiti's Cholera Outbreak Highlights Clean Water Crisis

Ansel Herz

Ansel Herz is a journalist based in Port-au-Prince, Haiti, who has written for Reuters, Alertnet, Inter Press Service, and Free Speech Radio News. In the following viewpoint, he reports that Haiti, which was struck by a devastating earthquake in early 2010, is suffering from a severe cholera outbreak as of October 2010. Herz notes that camps constructed after the earthquake by relief agencies have only limited access to drinkable water. The prevalence of water contaminated with sewage, he says, has contributed to ongoing infections and deaths.

As you read, consider the following questions:

1. Why were the two patients who died in Lafiteau not counted among the officially recognized cholera deaths, according to Herz?
2. What does Herz say was the initial response of Catholic Relief Services (CRS) when a camp committee leader complained that toilets were clogged with human waste?
3. According to Herz, what percentage of camps in Haiti lack access to water, and what percentage have no toilets?

Ansel Herz, "Cholera Outbreak Highlights Clean Water Crisis," IPS, October 28, 2010. Copyright © 2010 by Inter Press Service. All rights reserved. Reproduced by permission.

Access to Safe Water

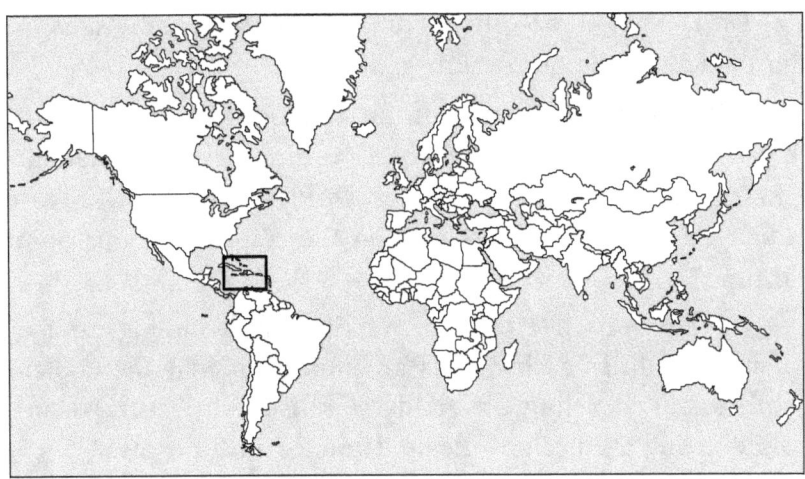

The man arrived from Arcahaie, near St. Marc in central Haiti where a cholera outbreak exploded last week [October 2010], initially overwhelming the local medical grid. It was an hour's journey to a hospital in Lafiteau, near the capital, where he died on Sunday.

Struggling with a Cholera Epidemic

"We tried to give him some liquids but it was too late," Dr. Pierre Duval told IPS [Inter Press Service news agency]. He said it was the second cholera death in three days. Five other patients who arrived from the epidemic zone showed the same symptoms: profuse liquid diarrhea and vomiting.

They looked gaunt and sickly on beds inside the tiny hospital's dimly lit patient ward, taking up one of its three rooms. Family members said they had bathed and eaten, then fallen gravely ill.

The two patients who died in Lafiteau are not counted among the 303 officially recognised cholera deaths in Haiti. A United Nations spokesperson said they were not "confirmed" cases of cholera because they occurred outside the epidemic zone and lab tests had not confirmed the presence of cholera bacteria.

Dr. Duval said no officials or medical teams had visited his hospital since the outbreak began.

"The mission is preparing for a nationwide cholera outbreak," the U.N.'s Office for the Coordination of Humanitarian Affairs spokesperson Jessica DuPlessis told IPS, before adding, "I'm sure there are gaps in the response at this point in time."

Haitian and U.N. officials are citing a dwindling number of new fatalities each day as an indication that the cholera outbreak is "leveling off" and "stabilised" in central Haiti, while saying the peak of the epidemic is still to come.

He said it was the second cholera death in three days.

"Affected zones are increasing. More capacities for implementation and coordination are needed" in central Haiti, according to a situation report by the St. Marc sanitation cluster of humanitarian groups. A video report by Al Jazeera English showed human waste from toilets at a Nepalese U.N. peacekeeping base running off into the river in Mirebalais, where there are over 50 confirmed cholera cases.

On Wednesday, a medical clinic operated by the charity group Samaritan's Purse in Cite Soleil reported treating a patient for "rice water diarrhea" and vomiting. The clinic's physician believes it to be cholera, according to an alert on the Haiti Epidemic Advisory System, an independent biosurveillance network.

The patient did not come from Haiti's central region, where the epidemic broke out, unlike the five cholera cases in the capital already confirmed by authorities. Cite Soleil is an impoverished slum on Port-au-Prince's northern tip, a 30-minute drive from Lafiteau. There are 20 cases in the capital under investigation, a Tuesday U.N. logistics cluster report says.

Hygiene and Water

Humanitarian groups say they are promoting hygiene and educating the capital's populace about cholera, which can spread easily through contaminated water and food. Some groups distributed soap in tent camps where 1.3 million people still live exposed to the elements nine months after the January [2010] earthquake.

"Some of them do nothing because of lack of funding," according to an internal overview of humanitarian activities by the water and sanitation cluster.

Charpon Davidson, 22, received soap from Catholic Relief Services (CRS) at Camp Carradeux, where at least 20,000 people live in tents and makeshift tarps. "They can't just give us soap as a solution. There are a lot of people already carrying the disease," he said.

"If we can't drink treated water, then we'll never have a solution to this sickness," Davidson told IPS. "Because where the problem started, in Artibonite, it's water—water that people take, they drink, they eat—where the disease started." Another woman asked the reporter if cholera was a natural disease or a poison from outside the country.

Camp Carradeux was battered weeks ago by a fierce storm that destroyed an estimated 10,000 tents. A walk-through of the lower camp showed that most families who lost tents, but not all, had received new ones. A few were given tiny backpacking tents that stand barely three feet off the ground.

"If we can't drink treated water, then we'll never have a solution to this sickness."

A chain-link fence was recently erected around an area in the camp where CRS plans to build 650 one-room structures called transitional shelters.

Down the road from Carradeux, a gate with a white Catholic Relief Services sticker faces the street. Inside is a sloped

Water

area crammed with about 300 families living under fraying tents and tarps, with a driveway in the middle running up to a second CRS-stickered barrier.

The camp is on the property of Catholic Relief Services just outside its materials depot. Humanitarian goods pass by the camp every day, but its residents have no water supply because their plastic water tanks are empty—just like a camp in Cite Soleil that IPS described in a previous report.

"We're inside the depot of CRS. Now, we're told to wash our hands before eating. The epidemic is present. CRS said they'd help us. They said that," said Jacques Pierre, the camp's committee leader.

In August, the camp's three pit toilets were full of human waste. At the time, Jacques told IPS his request for a functioning set of toilets was met with threats from CRS personnel to force them off the property. But after another aid group put pressure on CRS, construction began. They now have four working toilets.

"They started to do some small things, but actually what's necessary for us is water," Pierre said. "That's what is most important for us and for kids with diarrhea. The epidemic is becoming grave now, it may be just starting. So we need potable water to drink as well as food—these are most important for us."

Progress Is Slow

Asked if any organisation had come to educate them about cholera, Pierre replied, "No, we haven't seen any group come here and say anything to us. We've been ignored here in this space."

The Chronicle of Philanthropy reported in July that Catholic Relief Services had spent $30 million out of $140 million raised for earthquake relief in Haiti. Some $21 million came from the United States Agency for International Development

Access to Safe Water

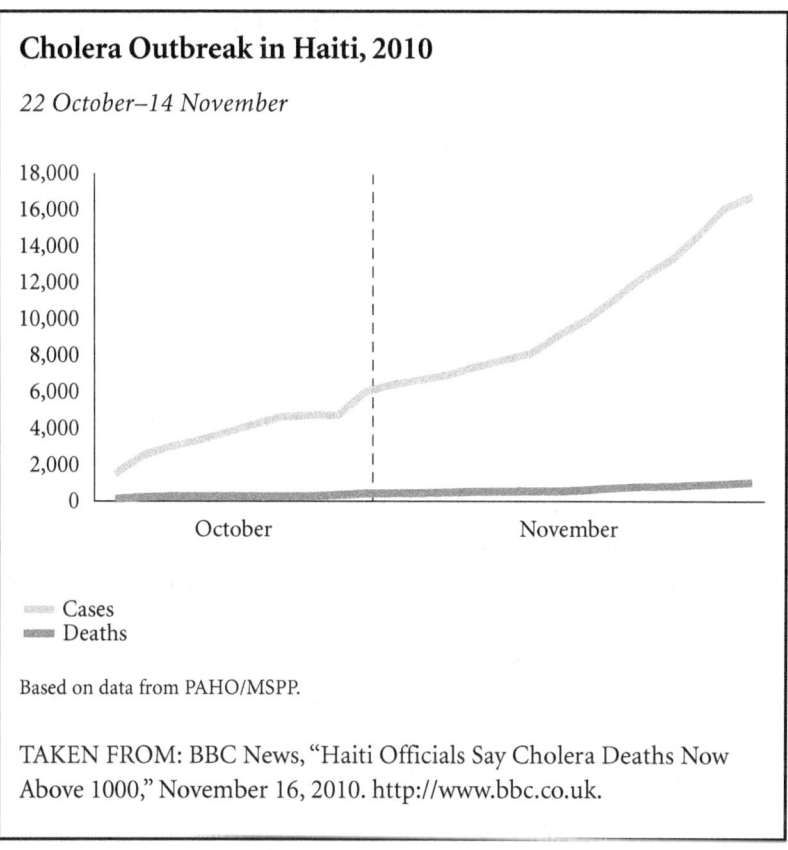

Cholera Outbreak in Haiti, 2010
22 October–14 November

Based on data from PAHO/MSPP.

TAKEN FROM: BBC News, "Haiti Officials Say Cholera Deaths Now Above 1000," November 16, 2010. http://www.bbc.co.uk.

(USAID), designated specifically for shelter, water and sanitation services in Port-au-Prince's displacement camps.

A senior member of another relief group, who requested anonymity, told IPS that CRS does not intend to install water purification systems in the camps until next year.

The percentage of the population without access to safe drinking water increased by seven percent from 1990 to 2005.

"That seems like a long time for someone living in the camps," the aid worker said. "The situation on the ground has been a ticking bomb waiting to go off."

Water

The water and sanitation coordinator for CRS confirmed it has no plans to install water purification systems in camps at this time, but is delivering extra-chlorinated water to some camps by truck. A joint report in September by the City University of New York's Haiti Initiative and Haiti's Faculty of Ethnology found that 40 percent of camps don't have access to water and 30 percent have no toilets.

But it's not just Port-au-Prince's makeshift camps that urgently need water. The percentage of the population without access to safe drinking water increased by seven percent from 1990 to 2005, according to a 2008 report by Partners In Health, a medical organisation currently responding to the cholera outbreak in Haiti's central region.

"Combined with unsanitary conditions, the lack of water is a major factor in exacerbating Haiti's health crises," the report notes.

The Interim Reconstruction Commission of Haiti has approved only one water and sanitation project, designed to expand the public water supply in Port-au-Prince. It would cost $200 million over five years, but is only 57 percent funded by international donors at this time.

Viewpoint 3

Bangladesh Is Trying to Establish Arsenic-Free Wells

IRIN News

IRIN is a humanitarian news and analysis service with the United Nations Office for the Coordination of Humanitarian Affairs. In the following viewpoint, it reports that many wells in Bangladesh are contaminated with arsenic. IRIN says arsenic exposure can result in illness and prolonged exposure can cause death. It can also lead to cancer. IRIN says health organizations and the government are attempting to address the problem by distributing medicine, testing wells, and making new water sources available. IRIN concludes, however, that millions of people in Bangladesh are still using water contaminated with arsenic.

As you read, consider the following questions:

1. According to WHO, what are the effects of drinking arsenic-contaminated water over a long period, as reported by the author?
2. According to IRIN, what is the approved global health standard for acceptable levels of arsenic in drinking water, and how does this differ from the Bangladesh standard?
3. The poisoning in Bangladesh stemmed from the creation of what, according to IRIN?

IRIN News, "Bangladesh: Arsenic-Free Drinking Water by 2013?," February 2, 2009. Copyright © 2009 IRIN. Reproduced by permission.

Water

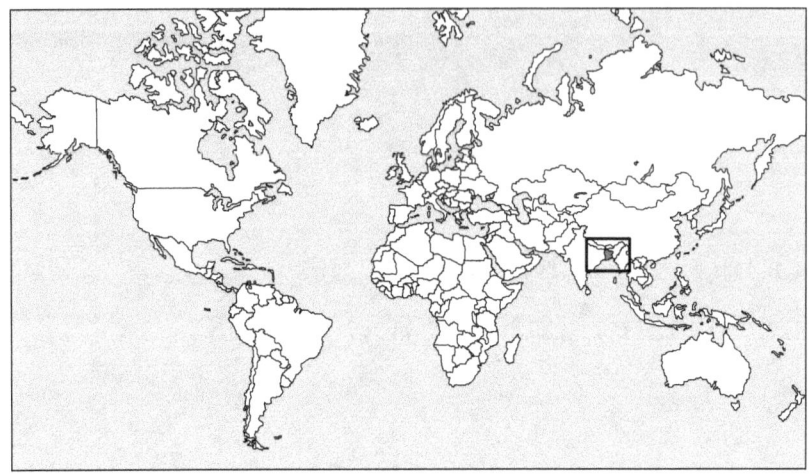

The government of Bangladesh has reaffirmed its goal to make the country's drinking water arsenic free by 2013.

Mass Poisoning

"Safe drinking water is a major problem in Bangladesh. We have to use more chemicals for more agricultural production to feed more people. Chemicals contaminate the water sources, so does arsenic. We will make the country arsenic free by 2013," declared Finance Minister Abul Maal Abdul Muhit on 30 January [2009] at the biennial conference of the Bangladesh Chemical Society.

Dhaka [the capital] has placed added emphasis on research and innovative technology to address the issue, as well as additional financial resources, he said.

His words come as more than 2,000 residents in the village of Garchapra, Alamdanga sub-district in Chuadanga District, fear developing arsenicosis after years of drinking contaminated water.

A recent survey conducted by the Department of Public Health Engineering (DPHE) and the Chuadanga District Health Office has confirmed 130 arsenicosis cases in the village.

Tube wells [in which long, wide, stainless steel pipes are bored into an underground aquifer] in the area showed high concentrations of arsenic. Seven members of one family are now feared to have died from arsenicosis over the past 10 years—a development that has left residents worried.

"Everyone thinks he or she might become the next victim of arsenicosis and die," Asirul Islam, chairman of Jehala Union (local government unit at community level), said.

So high are arsenic levels in Bangladesh that the World Health Organization (WHO) has described it as "the largest mass poisoning of a population in history".

Naturally occurring arsenic-contaminated water was first detected in Bangladesh in 1993 and is largely attributed to arsenic-rich material in the region's river systems, deposited over thousands of years along with sands and gravels, the UN Children's Fund (UNICEF) says.

According to WHO, drinking arsenic-rich water over a long period results in various health effects including skin problems (such as colour changes to the skin, and hard patches on the palms and soles of the feet); skin cancer; cancers of the bladder, kidney and lung; diseases of the blood vessels in legs and feet; and possibly also diabetes, high blood pressure and reproductive disorders.

So high are arsenic levels in Bangladesh that the World Health Organization (WHO) has described it as "the largest mass poisoning of a population in history".

To address those fears in Garchapra, DPHE officials visited the community and approved 10 tube wells for drinking water.

Additionally, the NGO [nongovernmental organisation] Forum for Drinking Water Supply and Sanitation—a national

NGO—started an arsenic mitigation campaign in the region and is busy distributing medicine for the treatment of arsenicosis patients.

Government health centres at sub-district level have also been assigned the task of distributing vitamin-fortified antioxidant capsules for patients.

"The patients are given a 30-day cycle of medicine and told to take one capsule a day. Patients with serious ulcers on their body are given salicylic ointment for external use," Bazlur Rahman, district health administrator of Chuadanga District, told IRIN.

Millions Exposed

In Bangladesh the acceptable level of arsenic in drinking water has been set by the government at 50 parts per billion (PPB) or 0.05 microgrammes per litre of drinking water, while the approved global WHO standard is 10 PPB.

More than five million tube wells have been tested since 2000. Twenty percent of the wells have been found to exceed the government approved limit of 50 PPB. One in five tube wells is not providing safe drinking water.

Out of 87,319 villages in the country, there are more than 8,000 where 80 percent of all tube wells are contaminated.

About 20 million people in Bangladesh are using tube wells with more than 50 PPB of arsenic, said a UNICEF document.

Health experts estimate that arsenic in drinking water will result in tens of thousands of cancer deaths in Bangladesh.

A British Geological Survey (BGS) study in 1998 on shallow tube wells in 61 districts found 46 percent of the samples contained above 10 PPB and 27 percent above 50 PPB.

It was estimated by the BGS in 2000 that the number of people exposed to arsenic concentrations above 50 PPB was 28–35 million and the number of those exposed to more than 10 PPB was 46–57 million.

Health experts estimate that arsenic in drinking water will result in tens of thousands of cancer deaths in Bangladesh.

The poisoning in Bangladesh stems from the creation during the last 30 years of millions of shallow tube wells usually less than 100 metres deep, and capped with a metal hand pump.

Many of the first wells were constructed as part of a programme to provide "safe" drinking water.

Although thousands of tube wells are known to be pumping arsenic-contaminated water, they remain the main source of drinking water for more than 70 percent of the country's 150 million-plus population.

VIEWPOINT 4

India Must Focus on Clean Water for Children

Craig Kielburger and Marc Kielburger

Craig and Marc Kielburger are Canadian children's rights activists and cofounders of Free The Children, an international charity and educational partner that empowers youth worldwide to become agents of change. In the following viewpoint, they note that many Indian children lack access to clean water. They argue that because children do not vote and lack political power, this issue has received less attention from India's government than it should. They suggest that India could address its water problems through rainwater harvesting, educational efforts, and point-of-use water purification tablets, as well as through long-term infrastructure efforts.

As you read, consider the following questions:

1. How many people in India lack sanitation facilities or access to safe drinking water, according to the authors?
2. What fraction of Indian children do the authors say will die from waterborne illnesses?
3. As reported by the authors, what results have been obtained when people have systematically taken actions to regenerate water in a region, according to Tom Palakudiyil?

Craig Kielburger and Marc Kielburger, "India's Children Don't Have Vote—Or Clean Water," *Toronto Star*, May 18, 2009. Copyright © 2009 by Free The Children. All rights reserved. Reproduced by permission.

Access to Safe Water

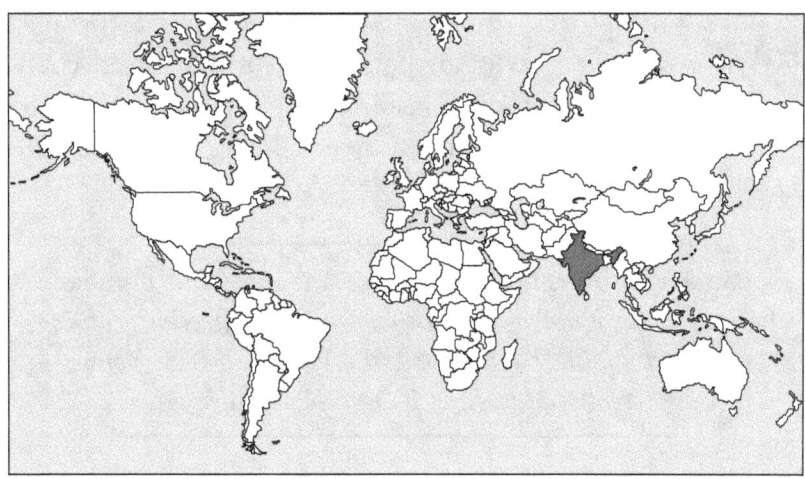

Surmaal used to be an enthusiastic student in his third-grade classroom.

Ignoring Water Access Issues

That was before his father passed away. Now, the 12-year-old is head of his household in the village of Lai, India. But, while he is shouldering an adult's responsibilities, Surmaal is still a child.

That made him too young to vote in the country's recent elections. His concerns went largely unnoticed.

For Surmaal and his family, getting water from the village hand pump is of vital importance. There are wells closer to his home but water depletion has caused them [to] run dry. So, Surmaal traverses two hills with the heavy buckets.

Like most people in the town, Surmaal would love to see those wells put back into use. That way, he could attend school again.

But, without a vote, it is not a high political priority. Water gets overshadowed by the economy and national defense. By ignoring this issue, which is affecting India's most vulnerable populations, the world's largest democracy isn't really addressing its nation's challenges.

"It's baffling that something so fundamental to people's lives is way down the list of political priorities for all countries," says Tom Palakudiyil, head of Asia region at WaterAid. "There is a huge amount of loss by not giving water and sanitation the attention it needs."

Water gets overshadowed by the economy and national defense. By ignoring this issue, which is affecting India's most vulnerable populations, the world's largest democracy isn't really addressing its nation's challenges.

A Complex Election Process Marginalizes the Rural, the Poor, and Children

The coordination [of] India's election is nothing short of extraordinary. It's a feat that involves thousands of candidates, five phases of voting and polling stations that eliminate geographic barriers for [the] country's 700 million eligible voters.

That incredible coordination doesn't translate to the treatment of water. India still lacks sanitation facilities for about 700 million people. On top of that, 200 million don't have access to drinking water. Those that do have no guarantee it is actually safe.

Still, water tends to get overlooked.

"Within the cities are where the affluent voters are, water is not such an issue," says Palakudiyil. "This issue touches the poor families. That's a vast number but it doesn't automatically translate into political dialogue."

The problem is that those being affected the most are not among the eligible voters—the children like Surmaal.

The Problem Can Be Solved

Surmaal is not alone in missing school to bring water to his mother and younger sisters. Millions like him perform the

> ## Water and India's Cities
>
> In the richest city in India [New Delhi], with the nation's economy marching ahead at an enviable clip, middle-class people ... are reduced to foraging for water. Their predicament testifies to the government's astonishing inability to deliver the most basic services to its citizens at a time when India asserts itself as a global power....
>
> A soaring population, the warp-speed sprawl of cities, and a vast and thirsty farm belt have all put new strains on a feeble, ill-kept public water and sanitation network....
>
> Today the problems threaten India's ability to fortify its sagging farms, sustain its economic growth and make its cities healthy and habitable.
>
> *Somini Sengupta,*
> *"In Teeming India, Water Crisis Means Dry Pipes and Foul Sludge,"*
> *New York Times, September 29, 2006. www.nytimes.com.*

same chores each day. All are at risk of waterborne illnesses like typhoid, dysentery and diarrhea. In fact, one in nine children will die before their fifth birthday largely due to illnesses like these.

But, it doesn't have to be this way. The solutions to India's water problems are within grasp. It just takes a coordinated effort to actually make it happen.

While a move towards better water infrastructure is more long term, there are options to help alleviate the water shortage now.

"Where people have systematically gone about taking actions to regenerate water in a region, after two or three years of community efforts, there is greenery and wells start to hold water again," says Palakudiyil. "If the communities come together, we can improve the water and keep it safe."

While a move towards better water infrastructure is more long term, there are options to help alleviate the water shortage now.

The communities in which Palakudiyil works have been able to conserve water through rainwater harvesting and educational efforts. As well, point-of-use water purification tablets can eliminate the risk of disease through contaminated water. Currently, these tablets are not widely available. But, through increased distribution efforts, these effective and inexpensive treatments could be sold at shops and kiosks in towns across the country.

"If the communities come together, we can improve the water situation and keep it safe," says Palakudiyil.

These solutions are doable. We just need the political will to stand up for those, like Surmaal, who don't have a vote. India successfully coordinated an election involving 700 million participants. Now, it needs to put that effort into bringing them water.

VIEWPOINT 5

Desalination Can Help Address the World's Clean Water Shortage

The Economist

The Economist *is a British business and political magazine. In the following viewpoint, the author explains that desalination, or removing salt from seawater, is one way to help address the worldwide need for clean water. The author notes that new technology has made the process more affordable and less environmentally damaging. Desalination remains expensive, however, and there may be a limit to how much the technology will improve. The author concludes that desalination can mitigate some water problems, but that it is unlikely to solve all the world's water problems.*

As you read, consider the following questions:

1. According to the *Economist*, how many desalination plants are in operation around the world, and how much drinkable water do they produce a day?
2. Why did reverse osmosis first become established as a way to treat brackish water, according to the *Economist*?
3. What discharge problems does the *Economist* say may be associated with desalination plants?

The Economist, "Case History: Tapping the Oceans," June 5, 2008. Copyright © 2008 by The Economist Newspaper Limited. All rights reserved. Reproduced by permission.

There are vast amounts of water on earth. Unfortunately, over 97% of it is too salty for human consumption and only a fraction of the remainder is easily accessible in rivers, lakes, or groundwater. Climate change, droughts, growing population, and increasing industrial demand are straining the available supplies of freshwater. More than 1 billion people live in areas where water is scarce, according to the United Nations, and that number could increase to 1.8 billion by 2025.

Limitless Water

One time-tested but expensive way to produce drinking water is desalination: removing dissolved salts from sea and brackish water. Its appeal is obvious. The world's oceans, in particular, present a virtually limitless and drought-proof supply of water. "If we could ever competitively—at a cheap rate—get fresh water from salt water," observed President John Kennedy nearly 50 years ago, "that would be in the long-range interest of humanity, and would really dwarf any other scientific accomplishment."

According to the latest figures from the International Desalination Association, there are now 13,080 desalination plants in operation around the world. Together they have the capacity to produce up to 55.6m [million] cubic metres of drinkable water a day—a mere 0.5% of global water use. About half of the capacity is in the Middle East. Because desalination requires large amounts of energy and can cost several times as much as treating river or groundwater, its use in the past was largely confined to wealthy oil-rich nations, where energy is cheap and water is scarce.

But now things are changing. As more parts of the world face prolonged droughts or water shortages, desalination is on the rise. In California alone some 20 seawater-desalination plants have been proposed, including a $300m facility near San Diego. Several Australian cities are planning or constructing huge desalination plants, with the biggest, near Melbourne, expected to cost about $2.9 billion. Even London is building one. According to projections from Global Water Intelligence, a market-research firm, worldwide desalination capacity will nearly double between now and 2015.

Not everyone is happy about this. Some environmental groups are concerned about the energy the plants will use, and the greenhouse gases they will spew out. A large desalination plant can suck up enough electricity in one year to power more than 30,000 homes.

As more parts of the world face prolonged droughts or water shortages, desalination is on the rise.

Costs Are Falling

The good news is that advances in technology and manufacturing have reduced the cost and energy requirements of desalination. And many new plants are being held to strict environmental standards. One recently built plant in Perth, Australia, runs on renewable energy from a nearby wind farm. In addition, its modern seawater-intake and waste-discharge systems minimise the impact on local marine life. Jason Antenucci, deputy director of the Centre for Water Research at the University of Western Australia in Perth, says the facility has "set a benchmark for other plants in Australia."

References to removing salt from seawater can be found in stories and legends dating back to ancient times. But the first concerted efforts to produce drinking water from seawater were not until the 16th century, when European explorers on long sea voyages began installing simple desalting equipment on their ships for emergency use. These devices tended to be crude and inefficient, and boiled seawater above a stove or furnace.

An important advance in desalination came from the sugar industry. To produce crystalline sugar, large amounts of fuel were needed to heat the sugar sap and evaporate the water it contained. Around 1850 an American engineer named Norbert Rillieux won several patents for a way to refine sugar more efficiently. His idea became what is known today as multiple-effect distillation, and consists of a cascading system of chambers, each at a lower pressure than the one before. This means the water boils at a lower temperature in each successive chamber. Heat from water vapour in the first chamber can thus be recycled to evaporate water in the next chamber, and so on.

> *The good news is that advances in technology and manufacturing have reduced the cost and energy requirements of desalination.*

This reduced the energy consumption of sugar refining by up to 80%, says James Birkett of West Neck Strategies, a desalination consultancy based in Nobleboro, Maine. But it took about 50 years for the idea to make its way from one industry to another. Only in the late 19th century did multi-effect evaporators for desalination begin to appear on steamships and in arid countries such as Yemen and Sudan.

A few multi-effect distillation plants were built in the first half of the 20th century, but a flaw in the system hampered its widespread adoption. Mineral deposits tended to build up on heat-exchange surfaces, and this inhibited the transfer of energy. In the 1950s a new type of thermal-desalination process, called multi-stage flash, reduced this problem. In this, seawater is heated under high pressure and then passed through a series of chambers, each at a lower pressure than the one before, causing some of the water to evaporate or "flash" at each step. Concentrated seawater is left at the bottom of the chambers, and freshwater vapour condenses above. Because evaporation does not happen on the heat-exchange surfaces, fewer minerals are deposited.

Countries in the Middle East with a lot of oil and a little water soon adopted multi-stage flash. Because it needs hot steam, many desalination facilities were put next to power stations, which generate excess heat. For a time, the cogeneration of electricity and water dominated the desalination industry.

Reverse Osmosis

Research into new ways to remove salt from water picked up in the 1950s. The American government set up the Office of Saline Water to support the search for desalination technology. And scientists at the University of Florida and the University of California, Los Angeles (UCLA), began to investigate membranes that are permeable to water, but restrict the passage of dissolved salts.

Such membranes are common in nature. When there is a salty solution on one side of a semi-permeable membrane (such as a cell wall), and a less salty solution on the other, water diffuses through the membrane from the less concentrated side to the more concentrated side. This process, which tends to equalise the saltiness of the two solutions, is called osmosis. Researchers wondered whether osmosis could be reversed by applying pressure to the more concentrated solution, causing water molecules to diffuse through the membrane and leave behind even more highly concentrated brine.

Initial efforts showed only limited success, producing tiny amounts of freshwater. That changed in 1960, when Sidney Loeb and Srinivasa Sourirajan of UCLA hand-cast their own membranes from cellulose acetate, a polymer used in photographic film. Their new membranes boasted a dramatically improved flux (the rate at which water molecules diffuse through a membrane of a given size) leading, in 1965, to a small "reverse osmosis" plant for desalting brackish water in Coalinga, California.

The energy requirements for thermal desalination do not much depend on the saltiness of the source water, but the energy needed for reverse osmosis is directly related to the concentration of dissolved salts. The saltier the water, the higher the pressure it takes (and hence the more energy you need) to push water through a membrane in order to leave behind the salt. Seawater generally contains 33–37 grams of dissolved solids per litre. To turn it into drinking water, nearly 99% of these salts must be removed. Because brackish water contains less salt than seawater, it is less energy-intensive, and thus less expensive, to process. As a result, reverse osmosis first became established as a way to treat brackish water.

The first big municipal seawater plant, which began operating in Jeddah, Saudi Arabia, in 1980, required more than 8 kilowatt-hours (kWh) to produce one cubic metre of drinking water.

Another important distinction is that reverse osmosis, unlike thermal desalination, calls for extensive pre-treatment of the feed water. Reverse-osmosis plants use filters and chemicals to remove particles that could clog up the membranes, and the membranes must also be washed periodically to reduce scaling and fouling.

In the late 1970s John Cadotte of America's Midwest Research Institute and the FilmTec Corporation created a much-improved membrane by using a special cross-linking reaction between two chemicals atop a porous backing material. His composite membrane consisted of a very thin layer of polyamide, to perform the separation, and a sturdy support beneath it. Thanks to the membrane's improved water flux, and its ability to tolerate pH and temperature variations, it went on to dominate the industry. At around the same time, the first reverse-osmosis plants for seawater began to appear. These early plants needed a lot of energy. The first big municipal seawater plant, which began operating in Jeddah, Saudi Ara-

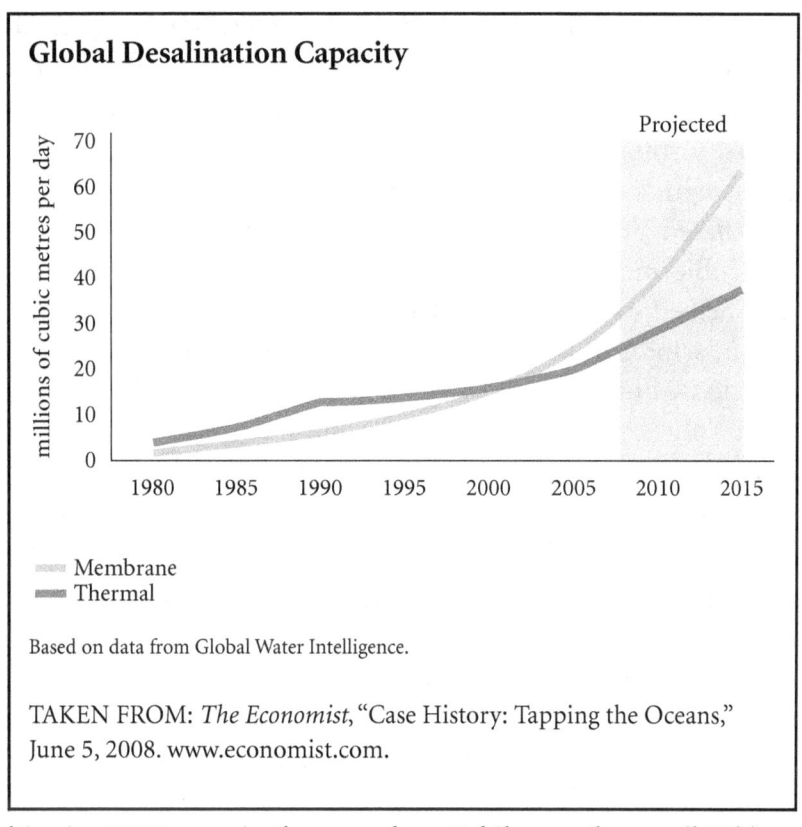

bia, in 1980, required more than 8 kilowatt-hours (kWh) to produce one cubic metre of drinking water.

Energy Recovery Increases Efficiency

The energy consumption of such plants has since fallen dramatically, thanks in large part to energy-recovery devices. High-pressure pumps force seawater against a membrane, which is typically arranged in a spiral inside a tube, to increase the surface area exposed to the incoming water and optimize the flux through the membrane. About half of the water emerges as freshwater on the other side. The remaining liquid, which contains the leftover salts, shoots out of the system at high pressure. If that high-pressure waste stream is run through a turbine or rotor, energy can be recovered and used to pressurise the incoming seawater.

The energy-recovery devices in the 1980s were only about 75% efficient, but newer ones can recover about 96% of the energy from the waste stream. As a result, the energy use for reverse-osmosis seawater desalination has fallen. The Perth plant, which uses technology from Energy Recovery Inc., a firm based in California, consumes only 3.7kWh to produce one cubic metre of drinking water, according to Gary Crisp, who helped to oversee the plant's design for the Water Corporation, a local utility. Thermal plants suck up nearly as much electricity, but also need large amounts of steam. "A thermal plant only is practical if you can build it in such a way that it can take advantage of very low-cost or waste heat," says Tom Pankratz, a water consultant based in Texas, who is also a board member of the International Desalination Association.

Economies of scale, better membranes and improved energy recovery have helped to bring down the cost of reverse-osmosis seawater desalination. Although the cost of desalination plants and their water depends on where they are, as well as the local costs of capital and operations, prices decreased from roughly $1.50 a cubic metre in the early 1990s to around 50 cents in 2003, says Mr Pankratz. As a result, reverse osmosis is preferred for most modern seawater desalination (though rising energy and commodity prices mean the cost per cubic metre has now risen to around 75 cents). Experts reckon that further gains in energy efficiency, and hence cost reductions, will be increasingly difficult, however. According to a recent report on desalination from America's National Research Council, energy use is unlikely to be reduced by much more than 15% below today's levels—though that would still be worthwhile, it concludes.

To achieve these reductions, researchers want to find better membranes that allow water to pass through more easily and are less likely to get clogged up. Eric Hoek and his colleagues from UCLA, for example, have developed a membrane embedded with tiny particles containing narrow flow channels, producing a significant increase in water flux. The membrane's smooth surface is also expected to make it harder for bacteria to latch onto. Depending on a plant's design, the new membranes could reduce total energy consumption by as much as 20%, reckons Dr Hoek. The technology is being commercialised by NanoH20, a company on UCLA's campus.

Meanwhile, the possibility of making membranes out of carbon nanotubes, which consist of sheets of carbon atoms rolled up into tubes, has also garnered attention. A study published in the journal *Science* in 2006 demonstrated unexpectedly high water-flow rates. But insiders think it will be a decade before the idea is ready for commercialisation.

Economies of scale, better membranes and improved energy recovery have helped to bring down the cost of reverse-osmosis seawater desalination.

Environmental Impacts

As desalination becomes more widespread, its environmental impacts, including the design of intake and discharge structures, are coming under increased scrutiny. Some of the damage can be mitigated fairly easily. Reducing the intake velocity enables most fish species and other mobile marine life to swim away from the intake system, though small animals, such as plankton or fish larvae, may still get caught in the intake screens or sucked into the plant.

A bigger problem may be the leftover brine, which typically contains twice as much salt as seawater and is discharged back into the ocean. So far little scientific information exists about its long-term effects. In the past, most big seawater-desalination plants were built in places that did not conduct adequate environmental assessments, says Peter Gleick, president of the Pacific Institute, a think tank based in California that published a report on desalination in 2006. But as plants are built in areas with tighter environmental restrictions, more information is becoming available.

Some recent measurements from Perth are encouraging. Initially scientists from the Centre for Water Research feared that the brine discharge from the plant would increase the saltiness of the coastal environment. But a monitoring study found that salinity returns to normal levels within about 500 metres of the plants' discharge units. "The brine discharge is a problem that can be overcome with good design," says Dr Antenucci.

Based on the limited evidence available to date, it appears that desalination may actually be less environmentally harmful than some other water-supply options.

A separate problem may be that some metals or chemicals leach into the brine. Thermal-desalination plants are prone to corrosion, and may shed traces of heavy metals, such as copper, into the waste stream. Reverse-osmosis plants, for their part, use chemicals during the pre-treatment and cleaning of the membranes, some of which may end up in the brine. Modern plants, however, remove most of the chemicals from the water before it is discharged. And new approaches to pre-treatment may reduce or eliminate the need for some chemicals.

Based on the limited evidence available to date, it appears that desalination may actually be less environmentally harmful than some other water-supply options, such as diverting large amounts of freshwater from rivers, for example, which can lead to severe reductions in local fish populations. But uncertainties over the environmental impacts of desalination make it hard to draw definite conclusions, the National Research Council concluded. Its report suggested that further research on the environmental impacts of desalination, and how to mitigate them, should be a high priority.

An Option, but Not Solution

The reverse-osmosis process is increasingly being used not just for desalination, but to recycle wastewater, too. In Orange County, California, reclaimed water is being used to replenish groundwater, and in Singapore, it is pumped into local reservoirs, which are used as a source for drinking water. In both cases the treated water is also available for tasting at local water-recycling facilities. This "toilet-to-tap" approach may leave some people feeling queasy, but wastewater is a valuable resource, says Sabine Lattemann, a researcher at the University of Oldenburg, Germany, who studies the environmental impacts of desalination. "Energy demand is lower compared to desalination," she explains, "and you can produce high-quality drinking water."

As water becomes more scarce, people will want to find several ways to secure their supplies. Many parts of the world also have enormous scope to use water more efficiently, argues Dr Gleick—and that would be cheaper than desalination. But sometimes, making desalination part of the approach to water management may be the only way to ensure a steady supply of drinking water.

In drought-ridden Western Australia, which ordered conservation years ago, the Water Corporation has adopted what it calls "security through diversity", otherwise known in the industry as the "portfolio" approach. At the moment, Perth's residents receive about 17% of their drinking water from seawater desalination. Desalination makes sense as one of several water sources along with conservation, agrees Dr Antenucci. But, he adds, "to say it is the silver bullet is wrong."

Periodical and Internet Sources Bibliography

The following articles have been selected to supplement the diverse views presented in this chapter.

Charitarian	"China's Water Crisis, Interview with Ma Jun, Environmentalist," January 18, 2010. www.charitarian.org.
The Economist	"India and Pollution: Up to Their Necks in It," July 17, 2008.
Emma Graham-Harrison	"China's Water Pollution Level Higher than Estimated in 2007," *Washington Post*, February 10, 2010.
Joe Mozingo	"Cholera Continues to Worsen in Haiti," *Los Angeles Times*, November 13, 2010.
Michael Schirber	"Why Desalination Doesn't Work (Yet)," LiveScience, June 25, 2007. www.livescience.com.
Somini Sengupta	"In Teeming India, Water Crisis Means Dry Pipes and Foul Sludge," *New York Times*, September 29, 2006.
Spiegel Online	"The River Runs Black: China Takes on Pollution—Sort Of," January 16, 2006. www.spiegel.de.
Julie Steenhuysen	"Arsenic Could Kill Millions in Bangladesh," Reuters, June 18, 2010.
U.S. Geological Survey	"Thirsty? How 'bout a Cool, Refreshing Cup of Seawater?," January 4, 2011. http://ga.water.usgs.gov.
Brian Walker	"Study: Millions in Bangladesh Exposed to Arsenic in Drinking Water," CNN, June 20, 2010.

CHAPTER 4

Hydropower

VIEWPOINT 1

In Uganda, Hydroelectric Dams Provide Needed Electricity

Christopher M. Walsh and Steven Shalita

Christopher M. Walsh is a communications consultant and Steven Shalita is a communications officer of the World Bank. In the following viewpoint, they report that construction on the Bujagali hydropower dam on the Nile in Uganda has begun. The authors argue that Africa faces an energy crisis, and they suggest that hydropower dams such as Bujagali can bring energy to a large percentage of the population. The authors say that environmental concerns should be taken seriously, but argue that they must be balanced with the need for electricity.

As you read, consider the following questions:

1. What has become a daily reality because of the electricity supply gap in Uganda, according to the authors?
2. According to the authors, President Yoweri Museveni says hydropower is a cheaper alternative than what energy source?
3. Where on the Nile is the Bujagali site located, as reported by the authors?

Christopher M. Walsh and Steven Shalita, "Uganda's President, the Aga Khan, Cut Ribbon on Bujagali Dam Project," International Bank for Reconstruction and Development/ The World Bank: web.worldbank.org, August 21, 2007. Reproduced by permission.

Hydropower

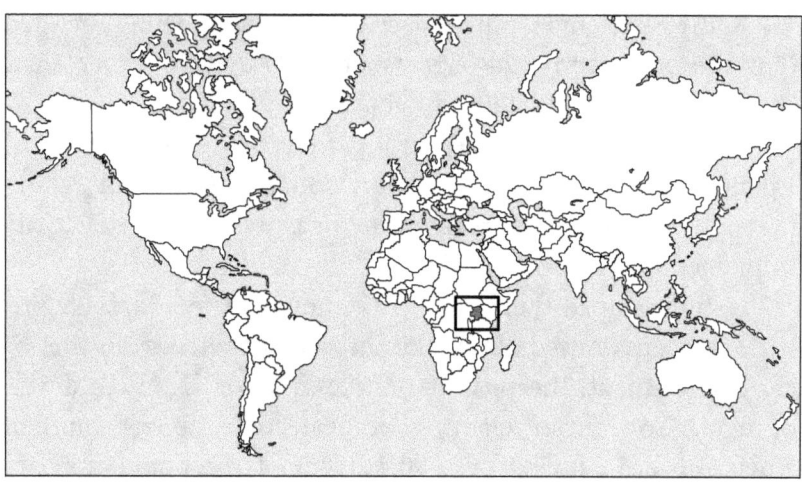

August 21, 2007, Jinja, Uganda—On August 21, Uganda's President Yoweri Museveni and the Aga Khan, Prince Karim al-Hussaini, spiritual leader of the Ismaili Muslims, laid the foundation stone for the Bujagali hydropower dam on the Nile River in a show of commitment to address Uganda's continuing energy crisis. The 250 MW project, co-financed by the World Bank Group, is a major component of Uganda's answer to an electricity supply gap that in recent years has made rolling blackouts a daily reality for Ugandan residents, businesses, and services.

The Aga Khan Fund for Economic Development supports the Bujagali project through its subsidiary development firm, Industrial Promotion Services (Kenya), which, along with Sithe Global (U.S.), comprises the project's development company, Bujagali Energy Limited or BEL.

With the Aga Khan at his side, Museveni urged other African leaders and development partners to face the reality that the continent suffers an energy crisis, which is not only the largest impediment to economic growth, but also at the root of major environmental and other development challenges.

Addressing environmental critics, the president reiterated that the environmental aspects of the Bujagali Project had been extensively studied and debated.

"I wish to assure the public that the Government of Uganda, working with the project sponsor, BEL, will ensure that all the identified mitigation measures are satisfactorily implemented," Museveni said.

He maintained that, while it is important to address legitimate concerns raised about the impact of the dam on the local environment, the project is necessary for Uganda's development. "You cannot claim to be protecting the environment when you are denying over 90 percent of the population access to electricity," he said.

Museveni said hydro power is a cheaper alternative than thermal energy, which is presently being used to address the power shortage.

> *"You cannot claim to be protecting the environment when you are denying over 90 percent of the population access to electricity."*

Bujagali is the largest single private sector investment in East Africa, the biggest independent power project in sub-Saharan Africa, as well as the largest single project ever funded by the International Finance Corporation (IFC) in the world, the Aga Khan said in his speech to media and others attending the event.

In April 2007 the IFC, the Multilateral Investment Guarantee Agency and the International Development Association approved US$360 million in loans and guarantees for BEL, the Government of Uganda, and commercial lenders to go ahead with the project.

Through its specially created Energy Fund, the Government of Uganda in July 2007 made available an advance US$75 million enabling work to commence while the lenders put together the required financing for the project. The government also provided US$17.5 million to implement the Resettlement Action Plan (RAP) for the Bujagali transmission line.

Bujagali is the largest single private sector investment in East Africa.

The Aga Khan noted the effort involved in getting the project started.

"It's not easy to attract traditional private investment capital for an ambitious infrastructure project in the developing world," he said. But "a long road of discussions and debates, negotiations and bids, adjustments and agreements with a wide array of partners" ended in success.

The project is expected to provide badly needed electricity, boost industry and provide employment for local people during the construction phase as well as later on in the industry and service sectors, according to Uganda's Minister of Energy and Mineral Development Hon. Daudi Migereko.

The Bujagali site is located roughly eight kilometers downstream from the source of the Nile in Lake Victoria and the existing Nalubaale and Kiira hydropower plants. As a run-of-river hydropower facility, the dam will re-use the water flowing from the upstream power plants to generate additional electricity.

The added power is expected to increase the supply to the national power grid at the lowest cost compared to other power generation options under Uganda's energy sector expansion strategy.

Uganda's energy strategy also includes a Power Sector Development Operation (US$300 million) approved separately by the World Bank Group in April 2007 that, among other things, provides funding for a set of investments and policy measures designed to reduce the supply-demand gap.

> ## Hydropower in Africa
>
> Hydropower is one of the cleanest and most reliable sources of energy. Environmentally conscious countries such as Canada, New Zealand, Norway and Sweden have chosen hydropower as their main source of electricity generation.
>
> Compared to other developing countries the level of access to electricity in Africa is very low, despite the continent's rich resources. Over 90% of rural population relies on traditional biomass energy sources such as wood, charcoal, crop waste, manure, etc., for cooking and heating, and candles and kerosene for lighting.
>
> The African continent is endowed with enormous hydropower potential that needs to be harnessed. Despite this huge potential, which is enough to meet all the electricity needs of the continent, only a small fraction has been exploited. This could be due to the major technical, financial and environmental challenges that need to be overcome for the development of this resource base.
>
> "Hydropower Resource Assessment of Africa,"
> Water for Agriculture and Energy in Africa:
> The Challenges of Climate Change, *December 2008*.

Support is also provided through three ongoing projects: the Power IV investment project (US$62 million), supporting improved power supply and government capacity to manage sector reform; the Energy for Rural Transformation Project (US$50 million), which supports the development of rural areas' access to renewable electricity; and US$40 million in investment guarantees for an electricity distribution company.

The Bujagali Hydropower Project has undergone extensive economic, environmental, and social due diligence. Documents made available to the public include the Project Economic Analysis—prepared by an independent consultant—and the Power Purchase Agreement. Consultations between BEL and communities surrounding the dam site have been ongoing throughout the project.

VIEWPOINT 2

In Brazil, Hydroelectric Dams Threaten Communities and the Environment

Joshua Partlow

Joshua Partlow is the South American correspondent for the Washington Post. In the following viewpoint, he reports that Brazil is planning to build dams on the Madeira River, a main tributary of the Amazon River, to generate electricity. He says the dam will damage a rich ecological area, hurt the fishing industry, and force the relocation of indigenous peoples. Partlow reports that Brazil plans to build many more dams in the Amazon basin to address its growing energy needs.

As you read, consider the following questions:

1. How much electricity does Brazil believe will be generated by the dams on the Madeira, according to the author?
2. How many families do the dam builders say will be displaced, and what are some competing figures, according to Partlow?
3. As reported by the author, who does Ivaneide Bandeira believe are living in the lands along the Madeira River, and what does she believe will happen to them if the dam is built?

Joshua Partlow, "Doubt, Anger Over Brazil Dams," *Washington Post*, October 14, 2008. Reproduced by permission.

Hydropower

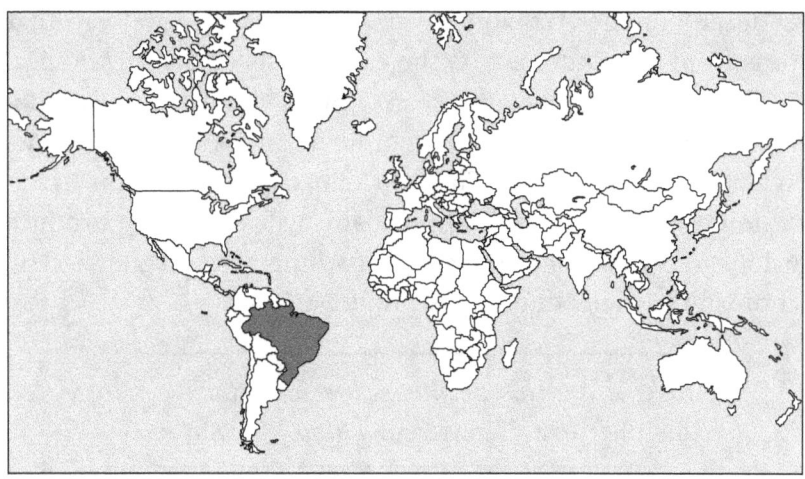

Porto Velho, Brazil—It is quiet here on the wrong side of progress. Hot wind blows dust across the dry bluffs. The brown river runs wide and placid.

In his painted wooden skiff, Francisco Evangelista de Abreu, a fisherman, motors up-current. Two river dolphins crest and submerge. His mind is elsewhere. The dam is coming.

"I don't know what's going to happen," he said. "I don't have any experience outside of this."

The task he and his neighbors are undertaking is to re-imagine their lives. They cannot stop the dam now. Once the waters rise, Jose da Silva Machado, 45, will no longer ferry schoolchildren across the river, nor fish in its rapids, nor live on its banks. Leonel Pereira de Souza, 61, insisted that his vegetable farm, where he was born, raised his children and grandchildren, is not for sale. Period. Yet he knows that conviction will dissolve in the flood.

"We are peasants. We live off the soil," he said. "They are offering houses in the village. There is no place to plant or fish."

Construction began late last month on one of two massive hydroelectric dams that are to span the Madeira River, a main tributary of the Amazon River and a major waterway that runs from the Andes across the rain forests of South America.

For the Brazilian government, this is prudent preparation, more than six years in planning, for a burgeoning economy's appetite for electricity. The two dams, the $5 billion Santo Antonio and the planned Jirau dam, will eventually produce 6,450 megawatts of electricity, according to the state electric company participating in the project.

The task he and his neighbors are undertaking is to re-imagine their lives. They cannot stop the dam now.

"We don't have any problems now. By the year 2012, considering the growth, the economic growth, we will need more energy, and this dam was made exactly to supply this future demand," said Marcio Porto, director of construction at Furnas Centrais Elétricas, the state company.

But the prospect of damming the Madeira has been widely criticized by social and environmental groups for its potential damage to the environment, river residents and nearby indigenous tribes. The Brazilian company working with Furnas on the Santo Antonio dam, Odebrecht, was recently expelled from Ecuador by the government for problems with a dam built there, which has raised further concern among critics of the projects in Brazil.

"It's extremely depressing to think that they're going to be able to build this dam," said Glenn Switkes, the Brazil-based Latin America program director for the environmental organization International Rivers, which has studied the Madeira dams. "This is an area that is one of the world's hotbeds of biodiversity."

The dam builders say that the reservoir created by the Santo Antonio will encompass 89 square miles, a relatively small area for a dam of its size, and that no more than 300 families will have to move. Organizations protesting the project, such as the local environmental group Ada Acai, estimate that 1,500 families will be displaced. The environmental impact study for the project put the number at 3,000.

In the Igarape Laje indigenous territory, a 265,000-acre area that is home to 400 people, the dam is a source of great worry. Indigenous leaders say the project will bring an influx of people to the area, harming hunting and fishing grounds and possibly turning the stilled waters into a breeding ground for diseases such as malaria, already common in this part of the western Amazon.

"Many people say the Indians are in favor of this project. This is a myth, a lie," said Arao Waram Xijein, 34, a teacher and local leader at the reserve. "We ask for the support of the world that they do not build these dams."

Ivaneide Bandeira, coordinator of Kaninde, a nonprofit group involved in indigenous issues in the Amazon, said traces of at least three uncontacted Indian tribes have been found in the lands along the Madeira River that could be flooded.

"How can the government give the license for a project without knowing if there are Indians there that might be flooded?" she said. "If these indigenous are not excellent swimmers, they're going to be killed. If this happens, it will be a genocide."

Many people say the Indians are in favor of this project. This is a myth, a lie.

Porto, the Furnas official, as well as federal environmental officials, disputed that any such tribes exist in this area. "There is no Indian reservation directly affected by the project," he said. "We did not find any isolated Indians in these studies."

There are at least four large hydroelectric dams already operating in the Brazilian Amazon, Switkes said, and the Madeira dams are two of at least 70 planned in the Amazon basin through 2030. The Brazilian government is finishing an

> ## The Environmental Impact of China's Three Gorges Dam
>
> For over three decades the Chinese government dismissed warnings from scientists and environmentalists that its Three Gorges Dam—the world's largest—had the potential of becoming one of China's biggest environmental nightmares. But last fall [in 2007], denial suddenly gave way to reluctant acceptance that the naysayers were right. Chinese officials staged a sudden about-face, acknowledging for the first time that the massive hydroelectric dam, sandwiched between breathtaking cliffs on the Yangtze River in central China, may be triggering landslides, altering entire ecosystems and causing other serious environmental problems—and, by extension, endangering the millions who live in its shadow.
>
> Mara Hvistendahl, "China's Three Gorges Dam: An Environmental Catastrophe?," Scientific American, March 25, 2008. www.scientificamerican.com.

environmental impact study on the Belo Monte dam, which would be the third-largest in the world, spanning the Xingu River in the central Amazon.

Damming the Madeira, in one of the world's most ecologically diverse areas, could affect more than 450 species of fish, according to environmental studies of the project. These species provide millions of dollars of income for the area's fishing industry.

"Brazil's energy planning is all about hydroelectricity, and most of that opportunity is in the Amazon," Switkes said. "These are huge, massive projects, and they're being pushed forward at this point because the government feels the Environment Ministry has totally caved in."

Hydropower

Environment Minister Carlos Minc said the companies building the dams have agreed to pay for the creation of two forest reserves and two Indian reservations, as well as give $30 million to improve the sanitation system in Porto Velho, which expects an influx of thousands of job seekers, and $6 million for environmental police in the area.

"The hydroelectric plants have an environmental impact—there's no such thing as zero impact—but if you don't do hydroelectric plants, you'll have to do thermo-electric plants with carbon and oil," Minc said in an interview.

> *"These are huge, massive projects, and they're being pushed forward at this point because the government feels the Environment Ministry has totally caved in."*

Some residents along the Madeira River have already moved out and razed their old homes, while others are contemplating the companies' offers of compensation. Several residents said they were concerned that the payments would not last indefinitely and not amount to what they were earning now as farmers and fishermen. Many felt they were not fully informed about what was about to happen to them.

"I live here. My children go to school here," said Abreu, the fisherman. "But if the state doesn't displace us, the water will. We don't know what to do."

VIEWPOINT 3

Wave Power May Become an Important Source of Green Energy in Europe

Mark Scott

Mark Scott is a correspondent in Bloomberg Businessweek's London bureau. In the following viewpoint, he reports that many projects to harness marine power are moving forward in different parts of Europe. Unfortunately, Scott notes, the marine power technology is still in the development stage, and marine power companies need assistance from traditional utility companies and from governments. Many investors, however, are still putting money into development in the hope that wave power and tidal power can generate significant energy with few environmental effects.

As you read, consider the following questions:

1. How much installed capacity from wave and tidal farms do analysts expect Europe to have by 2020, according to Scott?
2. Why does the author say partnering with traditional utilities is necessary for the marine power sector?
3. According to Scott, what renewables have snagged most investments to date?

Mark Scott, "Europe's Next Green Thing," BloombergBusinessweek.com, March 14, 2008. Copyright © 2008 by BloombergBusinessweek.com All rights reserved. Reproduced by permission.

Hydropower

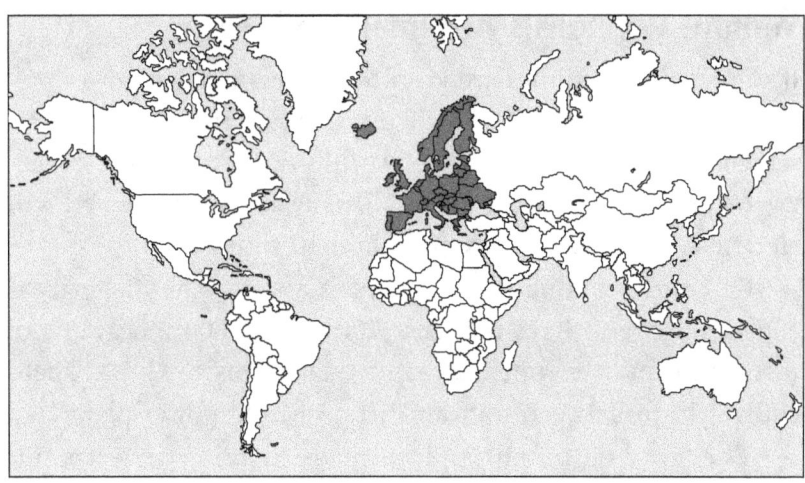

With oil prices hitting almost daily record highs and global warming climbing up the public agenda, the need for alternative energy sources has never been more urgent. But while wind and solar have dominated the recent rush to invest in renewables, market watchers reckon it could now be marine energy's turn to shine.

Ocean power—using the energy from waves or tidal flows to produce electricity—is quickly coming of age as a viable green resource that could help meet ambitious global targets to reduce greenhouse gases and dependency on fossil fuels.

European and North American power companies such as Canada's Emera Inc. and Germany's RWE are spending millions to fund wind and tidal projects. This investment has led to a new generation of more efficient technologies, with dozens of prototypes expected to be ready for commercial deployment within the next five years. "There's huge interest in both wave and tidal technology," says Thomas Boeckmann, clean tech analyst at market research firm StrategyEye in London. "It's gaining a lot of attention from energy companies, which will be able to offer financial backing and technical expertise to these start-ups."

Venture Capitalists Are Interested

It's no surprise utilities are keen to harness marine power. According to Britain's Carbon Trust, a government-funded research and advisory group, the world's oceans have the capacity to produce as much as 4,000 terawatt hours per year of electricity—enough to power Britain 10 times over.

Of course, getting to that point is a long way off. Analysts expect Europe to have between 2,000 and 5,000 megawatts of installed capacity from wave and tidal farms by 2020. That's equivalent to between four and 10 coal-fired power plants.

The growth potential is already driving investment. Dublin-based OpenHydro, for instance, has raised more than $80 million (€51.4 million) from energy firms and venture capitalists since 2005 to develop a new type of turbine that lies on the seabed and rotates to produce electricity as the tide rises and falls. Among its investors is Canada's Emera, which holds 7 percent of the company.

The world's oceans have the capacity to produce as much as 4,000 terawatt hours per year of electricity—enough to power Britain 10 times over.

Partnerships with Utilities Could Help

OpenHydro already has a 250-kilowatt prototype in the water off the coast of Scotland and plans to install a 1-megawatt plant in Canada by 2009. Chief Executive Officer James Ives says the biggest hurdle for marine power is persuading investors that it can consistently produce electricity. "You have to show that the technology is reliable even in the worst conditions," Ives says.

Analysts believe partnerships with utilities could help marine energy companies overcome these problems. For one thing, traditional power firms have vast experience in building

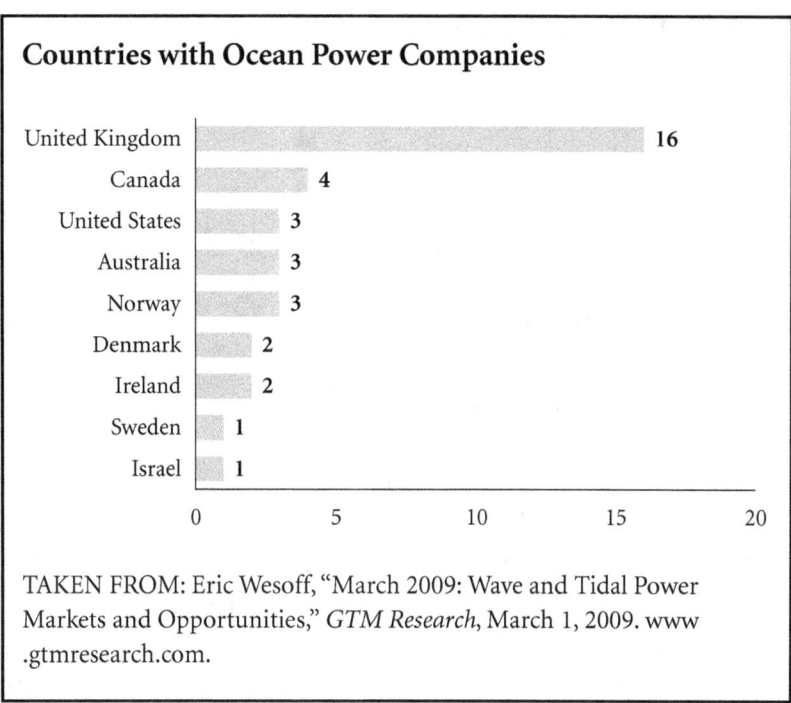

TAKEN FROM: Eric Wesoff, "March 2009: Wave and Tidal Power Markets and Opportunities," *GTM Research*, March 1, 2009. www.gtmresearch.com.

underwater power cables and gas pipelines. Deep-pocketed partners also could help shorten the gap between research and development and commercialization of marine technologies. "Cooperation [with utilities] is important because it provides a cash injection that shows power companies are taking the sector seriously," says Stephen Wyatt, the Carbon Trust's technology acceleration manager.

That's certainly the hope for Britain's Wavegen. In 2000 the subsidiary of Germany's Voith Siemens Hydro installed the world's first wave power facility to be connected to the power grid. The unusual prototype taps the wind—the strong breezes generated by waves—to drive generators located in a seaside structure. Wavegen is now working with the Basque Energy Board to construct a larger test plant on the northern coast of Spain, and a full commercial facility in Scotland should be up and running by 2010.

Part 2: Today's Wave Power Is Eco-Friendly

Of course, experiments with marine power have been under way for decades. One of the first plants in the world to harness tidal power, located in La Rance, Brittany, has been in operation since 1966. Built across the mouth of an estuary with powerful tides, the 240-megawatt plant produces electricity when tidal waters surge through turbines built into the barrier.

Today's experimental technologies tend to be more environmentally sensitive than those of yesteryear. Scotland's Pelamis Wave Power—formerly called Ocean Power Delivery—has created an eco-friendly "wave farm" off the coast of Portugal in partnership with Latin American utility Enersis (ENI) that already produces 2.25 megawatts of electricity.

Now Pelamis and Enersis, a unit of Spanish utility Endesa, aim to expand the site to 20 megawatts. Max Carcas, the company's business development director, also has targeted North America for growth and expects wave power to be a $10 billion-per-year industry by 2012.

Despite [the uncertainties], venture capitalists and power companies haven't stopped flooding the sector with cash in search of breakout technologies.

The Tide Is Turning

To be sure, there are plenty of risks for marine energy firms. High start-up costs, competition from other renewable sources, and investor fears over how well the technologies actually work could derail ocean power's move into the mainstream. What's more, generous and consistent government support will be essential to getting the industry off the ground. Marine energy currently costs at least 10 times as much as electricity produced by traditional sources. Countries like Britain and Spain offer subsidies for marine energy, but concerns that the support could be reduced has further confused investors looking to finance projects.

Despite this uncertainty, venture capitalists and power companies haven't stopped flooding the sector with cash in search of breakout technologies. Indeed, StrategyEye's Boeckmann predicts that thanks to growing investment, marine energy could constitute 20 percent of Europe's total renewable resources by 2020, compared with 40 percent from wind power.

That's good news for companies across the Continent hoping their projects could be the next big thing. Though wind and solar have snagged most of the investment to date in renewables, the tide is turning in favor of marine energy.

VIEWPOINT 4

In Portugal, Wave Power Projects Have Failed

Alan Copps

In the following viewpoint, Alan Copps reports that Pelamis Wave Power, an Edinburgh-based company working on a wave energy project in Portugal, has faced setbacks. He says these setbacks include equipment failure and financial collapse of one of the company's backers. Though Pelamis insists it will move ahead, Copps says the problems may discourage further investment in and experiments with wave power technologies. Copps is a reporter for the Times *of London.*

As you read, consider the following questions:
1. According to Copps, why was the deal between Pelamis and Eon notable?
2. What companies were involved in the Aguçadoura joint venture, according to the author?
3. What is the European Union's plan for the future of wave energy, according to Copps?

A pioneering €8m British green energy project has been halted because of a series of setbacks, including malfunctioning of the innovative equipment designed to turn wave energy into electricity and the financial collapse of one of the scheme's backers.

Alan Copps, "Wave Power Project Hits the Rocks," *Times* (UK), March 22, 2009. Copyright © 2009 by NI Syndication. All rights reserved. Reproduced by permission.

Hydropower

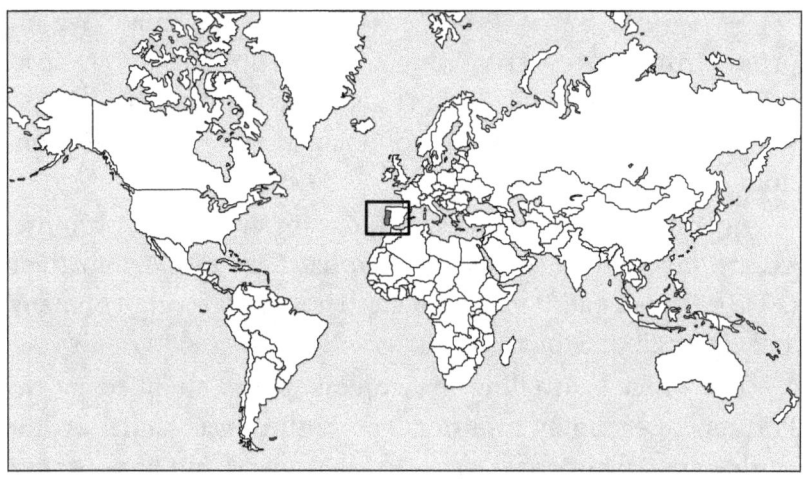

Pelamis Wave Power, based in Edinburgh, said its equipment had been towed back to shore in Portugal after it broke down. It will not be repaired immediately. Pelamis's wave-energy converters are considered to be the most advanced of their kind, and the future of the technology is now in doubt.

If the problems persist they could threaten a similar deal between Pelamis and Eon, the energy group. The partnership was the first instance of a big utility ordering a wave-energy converter for installation in British waters. The equipment was to be tested off Scotland next year.

Energy analysts say the difficulties over the Portuguese project, named Aguçadoura, call into question the viability of this type of wave power.

Pelamis's wave-energy converters are considered to be the most advanced of their kind, and the future of the technology is now in doubt.

The technical problems were compounded by the collapse of Babcock & Brown, the Australian company that has a 77% stake in the project and which went into administration last week.

"We are in limbo," said Max Carcas at Pelamis. "We are progressing and sorting out some problems on a cash-management basis. But we can't get the equipment back in the sea on our own." Carcas was confident the project would continue but could not say when.

Aguçadoura was launched amid a lot of hype last summer as a joint venture between Pelamis, Energias de Portugal (EDP), Efacec, the Portuguese electrical engineering company, and Babcock & Brown.

The official unveiling in September was attended by the Portuguese economy minister. The venture was hailed as "the world's first commercial wave-power project" and began transmitting electricity to the national grid.

Named after the sea snake Pelamis, each machine is 140 metres long, 3.5 metres wide and is partially submerged in the sea. The sections are linked by flexible joints and each section contains a hydraulic pump. The wave motion drives the pumps, which in turn work hydraulic motors that generate an electric current.

In the first phase, three Pelamis wave-energy converters were towed three miles out to sea with the aim of generating 2.25MW of power. If successful, a second phase was planned in which energy generation would rise to 21MW from a further 25 machines—enough to provide electricity for 15,000 Portuguese homes.

Even before the launch, though, the installation was plagued by problems. The date had to be set back after part of the structure sprang a leak.

In November, after two months of generating electricity, the three converter units developed further problems and the apparatus had to be disconnected from the grid and towed back to shore. Then came the news about Babcock & Brown.

Anthony Kennaway at Babcock & Brown said: "Our business is winding down over the next two years. Aguçadoura is one of the assets that we hope to sell.

"This is early-stage technology and you would expect the machines to be in and out of the water. It would be deeply disappointing if people start writing it off at this stage."

The failure of the Portuguese project highlights the problems engineers have in attempting to harness the power of the sea to create renewable energy.

The problems in Portugal cast a shadow over plans to repeat the experiment in trials at the European Marine Energy Centre in Orkney. Last month Eon announced that it had ordered a more advanced P2 machine from Pelamis which, at 180 metres long, is about 40 metres longer than the Pelamis units in Portugal. It will be built at Pelamis's Leith Docks facility in Edinburgh.

Both companies claim that the deal will go ahead. A spokesman for Eon said: "We still expect to be the first utility company to test a full-size wave-powered generating plant in UK waters. But we have to bear in mind that this technology is in its early stages. It's where wind power was a decade ago."

The failure of the Portuguese project highlights the problems engineers have in attempting to harness the power of the sea to create renewable energy. It could also put a question mark over the future of wave energy in the EU's plan to get 20% of its energy from renewable sources by 2020.

Ian Fells of Newcastle University, who has his own energy consultancy, said: "Wave power is very immature and very expensive compared with other renewable resources because you have to overengineer it to cope with extremes of weather.

"We have to get these things in perspective. Throughout the world wave power generates about 10MW of electricity. You would need something like 10,000 wave power units to replace one nuclear power station."

VIEWPOINT 5

In France, Tidal Power Has Been Successful

Robert Williams

Robert Williams is a writer for the British ecological magazine the Ecologist. *In the following viewpoint, he explains that France has had a functional and effective tidal power station on the river Rance since the 1960s. The station has provided reliable power with moderate, but not devastating, environmental consequences, Williams says. He concludes that as fossil fuels become more expensive, France's station may become a model for growth in tidal power.*

As you read, consider the following questions:

1. What were tidal mills, and when were they invented, according to Williams?
2. According to the author, how does the Rance tidal power station's power output compare to the output of nuclear and coal power plants?
3. What environmental problems does Williams say the tidal station has caused in the Rance estuary?

Although France is rich in many areas, it is very poor in energy resources. The Germans and Spanish have coal, Britain has enjoyed an abundance of oil, gas and coal, the Dutch have gas from the North Sea, and the Swiss enjoy plentiful hydro-electric power.

Robert Williams, "How France Eclipsed the UK with Brittany Tidal Success Story," *The Ecologist*, November 10, 2010. Copyright © 2010 by *The Ecologist*. All rights reserved. Reproduced by permission.

Hydropower

French coal mining ended in April 2004 with the closure of the last pit in the Lorraine region. Until the end of the 1970s, French natural gas supplied between six and seven million tons of gas per year, contributing up to 15 per cent of France's primary energy production, but this has now fallen to just 2 per cent, and oil production now stands at less than 1.5 million tons per year.

This lack of indigenous energy resources is, perhaps, a main reason why the French were conscious of the need for energy security long before the term became fashionable. This is also why France's energy policy has given priority to the development of a national, secure network of energy supplies, especially nuclear energy and renewable energies.

The French, as have other nations, have long looked to the power of the sea. French novelist Victor Hugo was very much on the right track when he said, 'Think about the movement of the waves, the ebb and flow, the to-and-fro motion of the tides, the ocean is a vast amount of lost power.'

The sea has actually been harnessed for centuries. Indeed, tidal mills were a medieval invention for milling grain, and were first mentioned as far back as the 12th century in both England and France. They became increasingly common until well into modern times.

These mills were built in low-lying areas, close to the sea. Dams containing swinging gates were built along shallow creeks. As the tide came in, the gates swung open inward, away from the sea. Water filled the area behind the dam. When the tide turned, the gates swung shut, forcing the water to flow seaward through the watercourse of the tidal mill.

The first attempt to build a large-scale tidal power plant in France was at Aber-Wrac'h in Finistère, the western-most part of Brittany, in 1921. Due to financial problems this attempt was abandoned in 1930. The plans for this plant did, however, serve as the draft for follow-on work.

[The] lack of indigenous energy resources is, perhaps, a main reason why the French were conscious of the need for energy security long before the term became fashionable.

The first studies for a tidal plant on the River Rance were carried out by the Society for the Study of Utilisation of the Tides in 1943. The main reason for choosing the Rance, which is on the north Breton coast between St Malo and Dinard, as a site for construction of the tidal plant was the fact that it had the advantage of having a huge difference between the ebb and flow of the tide, ranging from an average of eight metres to a maximum of nearly 14 metres.

In the 1950s the French started to put a major dam construction programme in place, although at the time there were no real success stories of harnessing tidal energy on a commercial scale anywhere in the world.

The construction of the Rance tidal power plant started in 1960. The project involved building a barrage 330 metres long in which the turbines were to be housed, a lock to allow the passage of small craft, a rockfill dam 165 metres long, and a mobile weir with six gates to rapidly balance the levels for the emptying and filling of the reservoir. The barrage was com-

Hydropower

pleted in November 1966 and was inaugurated by Charles de Gaulle. The plant was connected to the French national power grid on 4 December 1967.

In total, the plant cost 620 million francs—roughly 94.5 million euros at today's prices. The plant produces 0.012 per cent of the power consumed by France, with a peak rating of 240 megawatts for its 24 turbines. By comparison, a large coal or nuclear power plant generates about 1,000 MW of electricity. Annual output is about 600 million kWh, or an average of about 68MW. In spite of the high cost of the project, the plant's costs have now been recovered, and electricity production costs are lower, at 18 euro cents per kWh, compared with nuclear generation at 25 per kWh.

In the 1950s the French started to put a major dam construction programme in place, although at the time there were no real success stories of harnessing tidal energy on a commercial scale anywhere in the world.

Special reversible turbines were developed to be used in the Rance barrage. They can produce energy during both the rising and falling tides so that efficiency is increased. Two dozen turbines were installed each with a capacity of 10MW which makes for a total peak power of 240MW, enough to provide energy to 250,000 households.

Of course, a major drawback of tidal power stations is that they can only generate when the tide is flowing in or out—in other words, only for about ten hours each day. Since tidal flows are not absolutely precise, the plant does not generate electricity close to peak capacity throughout the year. However, the tides are predictable enough, so Électricité de France (EDF) can ensure that other power stations are generating sufficient power at those times.

Tidal barrages do have certain problems associated with them, particularly their effect on the environment. There has been some progressive silting of the Rance estuary. Species such as sand eels and plaice have disappeared, although sea bass and cuttlefish have returned to the river. Tides, obviously, still flow in the estuary and EDF endeavour to adjust their levels to minimise the biological impact. Sand Eel or sandeel is the common name used for a considerable number of species of fish. It is this potential ecological damage that concerns opponents of other proposed tidal power stations, such as at the recently abandoned Severn Estuary project.

If these opponents looked more closely, they could take comfort from research carried out in 1995 by the French National Museum of Natural History which showed that the Rance estuary continues to enjoy a rich and varied aquatic ecosystem. Although the construction of the dam modified the currents in the estuary, studies have pointed to a natural evolution of the sedimentary balance.

The Rance barrage is still the largest tidal power station in the world. It has generated reliable power for over 40 years and has never closed for anything other than scheduled maintenance.

The barrage has also been successful as a tourist attraction. The estuary now attracts water sports enthusiasts all year round. The barrage also created a transport link between St Malo and Dinard, cutting a 45km journey down to 15km.

In a future in which energy costs rise and the oil begins to run out, tidal barrage schemes could prove to be a major provider of strategic energy.

There is more interest in tidal power now than at any time in the past 20 years. Even as the UK government announced that the Severn barrage would not go ahead, Climate Change Minister, Greg Barker, on a visit to the Torrs Hydro scheme in the Peak District, called on enterprising communities to harness the power of their rivers and streams to generate both green electricity and money. He announced that former mills and water turbines which are brought back to life will now be eligible for financial support.

In a future in which energy costs rise and the oil begins to run out, tidal barrage schemes could prove to be a major provider of strategic energy. EDF has no immediate plans to construct further tidal power stations but the technology is proven and there is no doubt tidal power is substantial and ready to be harnessed.

VIEWPOINT 6

Tidal Power Is Not Economically or Environmentally Feasible in Britain's Severn Estuary

HM Government, Department of Energy and Climate Change

The Department of Energy and Climate Change (DECC) was created by the British government to address the challenge of climate change. In the following viewpoint, the DECC argues that a plan to harness the tidal power of the Severn estuary is not feasible. The DECC notes that building the necessary tidal barrages would be very expensive and would cause environmental damage to fish, birds, and the water of the estuary itself. The DECC concludes that other clean-energy options, such as wind power or nuclear energy, would be more efficient and less risky.

As you read, consider the following questions:

1. How much does the DECC estimate a tidal power scheme in the Severn estuary could cost?
2. What does the DECC believe would be the effect of an estuary in the Severn on local fish populations?
3. What are the advantages and disadvantages of the Cardiff-Weston barrage scheme, according to the DECC?

HM Government, Department of Energy and Climate Change, *Severn Tidal Power: Feasibility Study Conclusions and Summary Report*, October 2010, pp. 4–6, 8. www.decc.gov.uk. © Crown Copyright URN IOD/808.

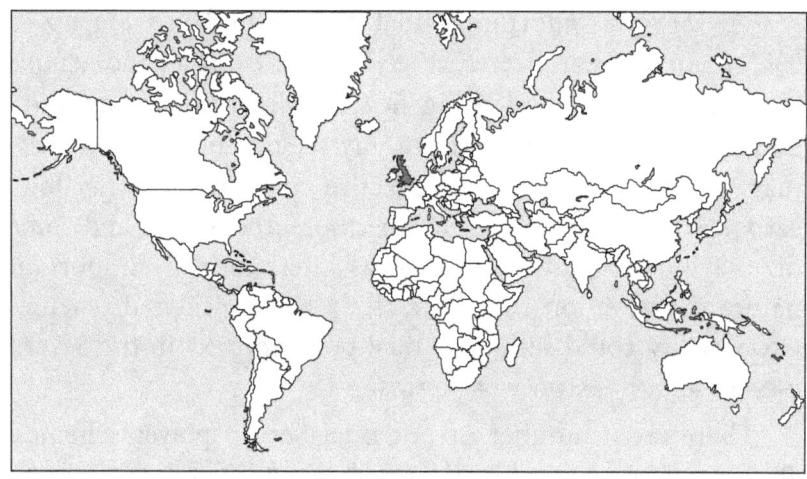

The UK [United Kingdom] must reduce its carbon dioxide emissions from energy and at the same time enjoy a secure and affordable supply of energy. We are legally committed to reducing our greenhouse gas emissions by 80% by 2050 and to meeting 15% of our energy demands from renewable sources by 2020.

Studying the Severn

Over the next decade, to achieve our renewable energy goals, the UK must increase the amount of electricity generated from renewables almost 5-fold on 2009 levels. DECC's [Department of Energy and Climate Change's] analysis shows that electricity will play a key role in helping to decarbonise our energy sectors and that overall electricity demand will increase to 2050.

Following a positive recommendation from the Sustainable Development Commission, a 2-year cross-Government feasibility study was launched to inform a decision whether or not to promote a scheme to generate electricity from the tides of the Severn estuary [in southwest Britain, forming the boundary between Wales and England].

Water

The Severn's enormous tidal range could provide up to 5% of our current electricity generation from an indigenous renewable source, and bring new employment opportunity both locally and nationally. But any scheme in the Severn estuary would need to be cost effective compared to other low-carbon energy alternatives. Furthermore, the Severn and some of its tributaries are designated as internationally important nature conservation sites. The study has considered whether Government could support a tidal power project in the Severn estuary and, if so, on what terms.

There are a number of potential Severn power schemes. Ten have been assessed by the feasibility study following a Call for Proposals during 2008. Half of these were judged to be unviable after public consultation in 2009 and were not included in the more detailed—but still high-level—consideration that followed. Over the last year the study has looked at the remaining 5 potentially feasible scheme options in outline and assessed their costs, benefits and risks. . . .

Any scheme in the Severn estuary would need to be cost effective compared to other low-carbon energy alternatives.

Key Conclusions

The key conclusions of the feasibility study are:

- a tidal power scheme in the Severn estuary could cost as much as £34billion, and is high cost and high risk in comparison to other ways of generating low-carbon electricity;

- a scheme is unlikely to attract the necessary private investment in current circumstances, and would require the public sector to own much of the cost and risk;

Hydropower

- over their 120-year lifetime, Severn tidal power schemes could in some circumstances play a cost-effective role in meeting our long-term energy targets. But in most cases other renewables (e.g., wind) and nuclear power represent better value. Moreover as a Severn scheme could not be constructed in time to contribute to the UK's 2020 renewable energy target, the case to build a scheme in the immediate term is weak;

- the scale and impact of a scheme would be unprecedented in an environmentally designated area, and there is significant uncertainty on how the regulatory framework would apply to it. The study has considered ways in which to reduce impacts on the natural environment and also how to provide compensation for remaining impacts on designated features. It is clear that the compensation requirement would be very challenging, however defined, and require land change within the Severn estuary and probably outside it also;

- a scheme would produce clearer, calmer waters but the extreme tidal nature of the Severn estuary would be fundamentally altered. This means that some habitats including salt marsh and mudflat would be reduced in area, potentially reducing bird populations of up to 30 species;

- fish are likely to be severely affected with local extinctions and population collapses predicted for designated fish, including Atlantic salmon and twaite shad. This could mean the loss of twaite shad as a breeding species in the UK as 3 of the 4 rivers where it breeds run out into the Severn estuary;

- water levels would also be affected and in order to maintain current flood protection levels in the Severn estuary additional flood defences would be required; these costs are included in the cost estimates for each scheme. In turn, such defences would provide longer-lasting protection to the affected areas;

- overall a scheme is likely to benefit the regional economy with net value added to the economy and jobs created. However these benefits would come at the expense of negative impacts on the current ports, fishing and aggregate extraction industries in the estuary;

- the Cardiff-Weston barrage [a dam-like structure] is the largest scheme considered by the study to be potentially feasible and has the lowest cost of energy of any of the schemes studied. As such it offers the best value for money, despite its high capital cost which the study estimated to be £34.3billion including correction for optimism bias. However this option would also have the greatest impact on habitats and bird populations and the estuary ports;

- a lagoon across Bridgwater Bay (£17.7bn estimated capital cost) is also considered potentially feasible, as is the smaller Shoots barrage (£7bn). The Bridgwater Bay lagoon could produce a substantial energy yield and has lower environmental impacts than barrage options. It also offers the larger net gains in terms of employment;

- the Beachley Barrage and Welsh Grounds Lagoon are no longer considered to be feasible. The estimated costs of these options have risen substantially on investigation over the course of the study;

- combinations of smaller schemes do not offer cost or energy yield advantages over a single larger scheme between Cardiff and Weston. . . .

- in addition, the study funded further work on 3 proposals using innovative and immature technologies. Of these, a tidal bar and a spectral marine energy converter[1] showed promise for future deployment within the Severn estuary—with potentially lower costs and environmental impacts than either lagoons or barrages. However these proposals are a long way from technical maturity and have much higher risks than the more conventional schemes the study has considered. Much more work would be required to develop them to the point where they could be properly assessed. Correspondingly, confidence levels on their yields, costs and impacts (including environmental impacts) are much lower at this point;

- many years of further detailed work would be needed to plan, finance, and assess the impacts of such a large structure as a Severn power scheme before a case could be put forward for planning consent. Even over a period of 2 years this study has only been able to consider feasibility and impact at a strategic level. If consented, the construction times would be between 4 and 9 years depending on the scheme. In addition, any of the schemes would first require new habitats to be created, or species re-introduced, to replace those that would be displaced. These habitats and measures require time to be effective; . . .

Costs and Risks Are Excessive

In the light of these findings the Government does not see a strategic case to bring forward a Severn tidal power scheme in the immediate term. The costs and risks for the taxpayer and energy consumer would be excessive compared to other low-

---

1. A tidal bar is similar to a barrage but more efficient; a spectral marine energy converter is a porous barrage that generates energy continuously rather than just during tides.

Water

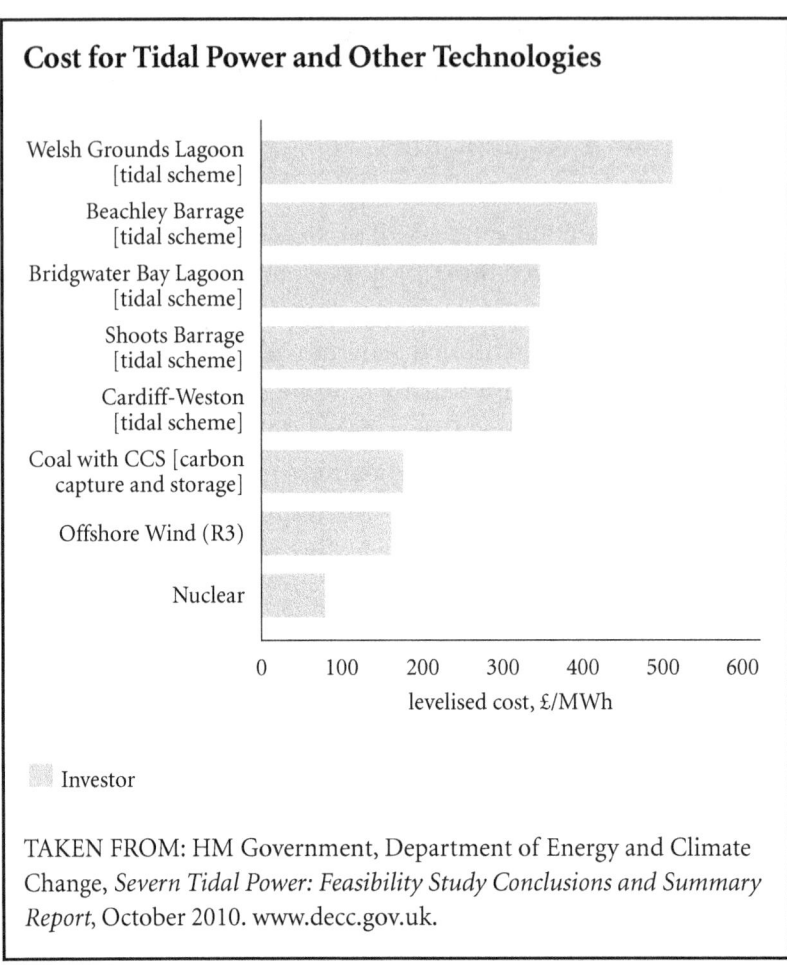

TAKEN FROM: HM Government, Department of Energy and Climate Change, *Severn Tidal Power: Feasibility Study Conclusions and Summary Report*, October 2010. www.decc.gov.uk.

carbon energy options. Furthermore, regulatory barriers create uncertainties that would add to the cost and risk of construction. The Government believes that other options, such as the expansion of wind energy, carbon capture and storage and nuclear power without public subsidy, represent a better deal for taxpayers and consumers at this time.

However, the Government recognises that factors which will determine the feasibility of Severn tidal power could change over time. There are circumstances in which a future Government may choose to review the case for Severn tidal power. . . .

The huge scale of a Severn tidal power scheme is unique. The development of tidal range options elsewhere in the UK is being considered separately by the private sector. While we hope the study will be useful to other feasibility studies, it should be noted that its conclusions do not bear on schemes outside the Severn estuary.

Periodical and Internet Sources Bibliography

The following articles have been selected to supplement the diverse views presented in this chapter.

Matt Chorley	"Severn Barrage Tidal Power Plan Axed," *Independent*, October 17, 2010.
Economist	"Tidal Power: Green on Green," January 29, 2009.
Economist	"Wave Power: The Coming Wave," June 5, 2008.
David Ehrlich	"Tidal Power Gets Modern in France," Cleantech Group, July 16, 2008. http://cleantech.com.
Gustavo Faleiros	"Brazilian President's Promises Crumble Under Weight of Belo Monte Dam," *Guardian*, February 1, 2011.
Mara Hvistendahl	"China's Three Gorges Dam: An Environmental Catastrophe?," *Scientific American*, March 25, 2008.
Michael Kanellos	"Wave Power to Go Commercial in California," CNET, December 17, 2007. http://news.cnet.com.
Tracy Loew	"Oregon Is First U.S. Site for a Wave-Power Farm," *USA Today*, February 17, 2010.
Matthew McDermott	"Portugal's Pelamis Wave Power Project Dead in the Water," TreeHugger, March 17, 2009. www.treehugger.com.
Solana Pyne and Erik German	"Belo Monte Dam: Brazil's Energy Gamble," GlobalPost, February 3, 2011. www.globalpost.com.

For Further Discussion

Chapter 1

1. Drew Warne-Smith and James Madden quote a Mr. Court, who has visited Australia's beaches for years and says he has noticed no rise in sea level. Do you think Mr. Court is a reliable scientific source? Why or why not? What reliable scientific information is there in the Warne-Smith/Madden viewpoint, or in the Kieran R. Hickey viewpoint, that might help you decide whether sea-level rise is a serious problem?

2. Based on the viewpoints by Severin Carrell, Matt Ridley, Paul Van Slambrouck, and Richard Grant, which seems like a more serious problem, ocean acidification or the Great Pacific Garbage Patch? Explain the reason for your answer.

Chapter 2

1. Do you think Alex Shoumatoff is blaming the inhabitants of Mali for the desertification? Why or why not? Would Mae-Wan Ho and Lim Li Ching argue that the inhabitants of the Sahel are responsible for desertification in the region? Explain your answer.

2. Clean water is available to everyone. Is this true? Based on the readings in this chapter, do the rich and powerful have more access to water than others? Explain your answer.

Chapter 3

1. Based on Andreas Lorenz, what interests or goals does China have to balance against its need for clean water? How well is it balancing those goals?
2. Would desalination (discussed in the *Economist* viewpoint) solve the problems concerning clean water in Haiti, Bangladesh, or India? Why or why not?

Chapter 4

1. Based on Christopher M. Walsh and Steven Shalita's viewpoint and on Joshua Partlow's viewpoint, would you like to have a hydropower dam built in your area? Do you think, in general, that hydropower is a good source of energy? Explain your answers.
2. Do you think that wave power or tidal power is likely to be a more useful source of energy in the future? Explain your answer.

Organizations to Contact

The editors have compiled the following list of organizations concerned with the issues debated in this book. The descriptions are derived from materials provided by the organizations. All have publications or information available for interested readers. The list was compiled on the date of publication of the present volume; the information provided here may change. Be aware that many organizations take several weeks or longer to respond to inquiries, so allow as much time as possible.

Global Water
3600 South Harbor Boulevard, #514, Oxnard, CA   93035
(805) 985-3057 • fax: (805) 985-3688
e-mail: info@globalwater.org
website: www.globalwater.org

Global Water is an international nonprofit, nongovernmental organization dedicated to helping provide clean drinking water for developing countries. The organization provides technical assistance, water supply equipment, and volunteers to help poor countries develop safe and effective water supply programs around the world. Its website explores water issues visually through a movie-for-instant-viewing, *Dying of Thirst*, and a slide show, *Live a Life That Matters*. It also has links and documents for download.

Intergovernmental Panel on Climate Change (IPCC)
IPCC Secretariat c/o World Meteorological Organization
Geneva 2   CH-1211
    Switzerland
(+41) 22-730-8208 • fax: (+41) 22-730-8025
e-mail: IPCC-Sec@wmo.int
website: www.ipcc.ch

The World Meteorological Organization (WMO) and the United Nations Environment Programme (UNEP) established the Intergovernmental Panel on Climate Change (IPCC) in

1988. The role of the IPCC is to assess information relevant to understanding the scientific basis of the risks of human-induced climate change, its potential impact, and options for adaptation and mitigation. The IPCC website includes press releases, global climate change reports, links, and publications available for download.

International Water Management Institute (IWMI)
127, Sunil Mawatha, Pelawatte, Battaramulla
 Sri Lanka
(+94) 11 2880000 • fax: (+94) 11 2786854
e-mail: iwmi@cgiar.org
website: www.iwmi.cgiar.org

The International Water Management Institute (IWMI) is a nonprofit, scientific organization funded by the Consultative Group on International Agricultural Research (CGIAR). IWMI concentrates on water and related land-management challenges faced by poor rural communities. Its website includes maps, publications, research reports, and documents for download.

UNESCO World Water Assessment Programme
Villa La Colombella-Località di Colombella Alta
06134 Colombella (PERUGIA)
 Italy
e-mail: wwap@unesco.org
website: www.unesco.org/water/wwap

The World Water Assessment Programme is part of the United Nations Educational, Scientific and Cultural Organization (UNESCO) and is designed to provide information related to global freshwater issues. Every three years, it publishes the United Nations *World Water Development Report*, a comprehensive review that gives an overall picture of the state of the world's freshwater resources and aims to provide decision makers with the tools to implement sustainable use of earth's water. The website also includes facts and figures, case studies, and other resources.

United Nations Development Programme (UNDP)
One United Nations Plaza, New York, NY   10017
(212) 906-5000 • fax: (212) 906-5001
website: www.undp.org

The United Nations Development Programme (UNDP) is the UN's global development network, an organization advocating for change and connecting countries to knowledge, experience, and resources to help people build a better life. The UNDP site includes publications such as *Beyond Scarcity: Power, Poverty, and the Global Water Crisis* and other documents available for download.

Water.org
920 Main Street, Suite 1800, Kansas City, MO   64105
(816) 877-8400
website: www.water.org

Water.org is a US-based nonprofit organization committed exclusively to providing safe drinking water and sanitation to people in developing countries. Water.org traces its roots back to the founding of WaterPartners in 1990. In July 2009 WaterPartners merged with H2O Africa, resulting in the launch of Water.org. The organization publishes *Ripples*, an annual magazine, and a monthly newsletter, which is available on its website. The website also includes annual reports, news, and other publications.

Water Supply and Sanitation Collaborative Council (WSSCC)
15, Chemin Louis-Dunant 1202, Geneva
   Switzerland
+41(0) 22 560 81 81 • fax: +41(0) 22 560 81 84
e-mail: wsscc@wsscc.org
website: www.wsscc.org

The Water Supply and Sanitation Collaborative Council (WSSCC) exists under a mandate from the United Nations. Its mission is to achieve sustainable water supply, sanitation, and hygiene for all people in the world. The organization focuses exclusively on those people who lack water and sanitation. The WSSCC website includes downloadable publications such as *Rights to Water and Sanitation—A Handbook for Activists*, as well as fact sheets, informational pages, news, and other resources.

World Bank—Water and Sanitation Program
1818 H Street NW, Washington, DC   20433
(202) 473-1000 • fax: (202) 477-6391
website: www.worldbank.org/water

The World Bank is an international organization that provides loans, grants, and technical assistance to developing countries around the world to help them reduce poverty and improve education, health, infrastructure, communications, and many other critical areas of national development. Its website contains news and information about global water issues under the topic "Water and Sanitation Program." This site has documents, research reports, and publications for download.

World Health Organization (WHO)—Water
Avenue Appia 20, Geneva 27   1211
   Switzerland
+41 22 791 21 11 • fax: + 41 22 791 31 11
e-mail: info@who.int
website: http://www.who.int/topics/water/en/

The World Health Organization (WHO) is an agency of the United Nations formed in 1948 with the goal of creating and ensuring a world where all people can live with high levels of both mental and physical health. The organization researches clean-water issues and disseminates information on the topic. The WHO publishes the *Bulletin of the World Health Organization*, which is available online, as well as the *Pan American Journal of Public Health*. It publishes reports on water including "Progress on Sanitation and Drinking Water 2010 Update" and "Guidelines for Drinking Water Quality."

World Water Council (WWC)
Espace Gaymard, 2-4 place d'Arvieux, Marseille   13002
   France
+33 4 91 99 41 00 • fax: +33 4 91 99 41 01
website: www.worldwatercouncil.org

The World Water Council (WWC) was established in 1996 in response to increasing concern from the global community about world water issues. Its mission is to promote awareness, build political commitment, and trigger action on critical water issues at all levels to facilitate the efficient management and use of water on an environmentally sustainable basis. Its website includes documents, research reports, new releases, case studies, and publications for download.

Bibliography of Books

Michelle Allsopp, Richard Page, Paul Johnston, and David Santillo — *State of the World's Oceans*. New York: Springer Science, 2010.

Roy H. Behnke, ed. — *Desertification: Causes, Impacts & Consequences*. New York: Springer, 2011.

Maggie Black and Jannet King — *The Atlas of Water: Mapping the World's Most Critical Resource*, 2nd ed. London: Earthscan, 2009.

Colin Chartres and Samyuktha Varma — *Out of Water: From Abundance to Scarcity and How to Solve the World's Water Problems*. Upper Saddle River, NJ: FT Press, 2011.

Deirdre Chetham — *Before the Deluge: The Vanishing World of the Yangtze's Three Gorges*. New York: Palgrave Macmillan, 2002.

John A. Church, Philip L. Woodworth, Thorkild Aarup, and W. Stanley Wilson, eds. — *Understanding Sea-Level Rise and Variability*. Hoboken, NJ: Wiley-Blackwell, 2010.

David Craddock — *Renewable Energy Made Easy: Free Energy from Solar, Wind, Hydropower, and Other Alternative Energy Sources*. Ocala, FL: Atlantic Publishing Group, 2008.

Barbara J. Cummings	*Dam the Rivers, Damn the People: Development and Resistence in Amazonian Brazil*, 2nd ed. London: Earthscan Publications Ltd, 2009.
Scott Davis	*Serious Microhydro: Water Power Solutions from the Experts*. Gabriola Island, BC: New Society Publishers, 2010.
Helmut Geist	*The Causes and Progression of Desertification*. Burlington, VT: Ashgate Publishing Company, 2005.
James Hoggan and Richard Littlemore	*Climate Cover-Up: The Crusade to Deny Global Warming*. Vancouver, BC: Greystone Books, 2009.
Bjorn Lomborg	*Cool It: The Skeptical Environmentalist's Guide to Global Warming*. New York: Alfred A. Knopf, 2007.
Jun Ma	*China's Water Crisis*. Norwalk, CT: EastBridge, 2004.
Andrew C. Mertha	*China's Water Warriors: Citizen Action and Policy Change*. Ithaca, NY: Cornell University Press, 2011.
Skye Kathleen Moody	*Washed Up: The Curious Journeys of Flotsam and Jetsam*. Seattle, WA: Sasquatch Books, 2006.
Charles Moore	*Plastic Ocean: How a Sea Captain's Chance Discovery Launched an Obsessive Quest to Save the Oceans*. New York: Avery, 2011.

Orrin H. Pilkey and Rob Young	*The Rising Sea.* Washington, DC: Island Press, 2009.
Binayak Ray	*Water: The Looming Crisis in India.* Lanham, MD: Lexington Books, 2008.
Peter Rogers and Susan Leal	*Running Out of Water: The Looming Crisis and Solutions to Conserve Our Most Precious Resource.* New York: Palgrave Macmillan, 2010.
Vandana Shiva	*Water Wars: Privatization, Pollution, and Profit.* Cambridge, MA: South End Press, 2002.
Hillel Shuval and Hassan Dweik, eds.	*Water Resources in the Middle East: Israel-Palestinian Water Issues—from Conflict to Cooperation.* New York: Springer, 2007.
Roy W. Spencer	*Climate Confusion: How Global Warming Hysteria Leads to Bad Science, Pandering Politicians and Misguided Policies That Hurt the Poor.* New York: Encounter Books, 2008.
Kenneth M. Vigil	*Clean Water: An Introduction to Water Quality and Pollution Control*, 2nd ed. Corvallis: Oregon State University Press, 2003.

Index

Geographic headings and page numbers in **boldface** refer to viewpoints about that country or region.

Numerals

1967 War, 95, 103

A

Accidents
    modern technologies, potentials, 54–55
    water pollution, 122–125, 127
Acid rain, 40
Acidification of oceans
    past and future, 36
    reports, 35–38, 40–41
    seriousness overstated, 39–42
    threats and dangers, 34–38, 59
Ada Acai, 167
Africa
    climate shifts and human action have caused irreversible desertification, 63–70
    famines, 66, 67, 68, 73
    human action reversing desertification, 71–79
    hydropower assessment, 162
    See also Lake Victoria; Nile River; specific nations
Afunaduula, Isaac, 114, 117
Aga Khan, Uganda. *See* al-Hussaini, Prince Karim
Aga Khan Fund for Economic Development, 159
Agriculture
    changes of hydroelectric dams, Brazil, 165, 169
    crop areas in the Sahel, 67*t*, 78

drinking water pollution, 136
India, 143
innovations and efficiencies, Africa, 69, 73–75
Ireland coastal erosion, 25
Ireland growing seasons, 21
Jordan River irrigation, 108, 110
Lebanese farmers, evictions, 96
Palestinian farmers, evictions, 95
Palestinian irrigation, 100, 101, 102, 105
See also Reforestation
Air pollution, 125–126
al-Hussaini, Prince Karim, 159, 160, 161
Albatrosses, 53, 55
Algae
    algal blooms, 112
    ocean acidification effects, 35, 37
Algalita Marine Research Foundation, 51
Alkaline pH, 41
Alps, 23
Amazon River, 164, 165–169
Andes, 23
Anemone, 37
Animals. *See* Marine life
Antarctic Circumpolar Current, 32
Antarctica, ice melts, 23, 32
Apartheid, 102–103

Aquifers
    coastal, and damages, 25
    Palestine, 97–98, 103
Aragonite, 38
Arctic seas, acidification, 38, 41
Arsenic-free wells, 135–139
Arsenicosis, 136–137
Artesian wells, 96, 98, 103
Australia, 27–33
    continental rise, 31
    desalination, 146–147, 152, 154, 155
    sea level rise potential has been exaggerated, 27–33
Australian Baseline Sea Level Monitoring Project, 30

B

Babcock & Brown, 177–178
Baekeland, Leo, 54–55
Baird, Brian, 38
Bamako, Mali, 65, 66
Bangladesh, 135–139
Barker, Greg, 184–185
Bauer, Carl, 90–91, 93
Baxter, John, 35, 36, 37
Beach litter, 51, 52–53
Beijing, China, 82, 85, 125
Bible, 107
Bicarbonate, 41, 42
Biodiverse areas, 166, 168
Biomass energy, 162
Birds
    estuary habitats, 186, 189, 190
    harms from plastics, 53, 55
    migratory pathways, 107
Birkett, James, 148
Brackish water, 149, 150
Bradshaw, Corey J.A., 15–16
Brazil, 164–169

Brine, 153–154
Britain. *See* United Kingdom
British Geological Survey, 138–139
Brittle stars, 37
Bromberg, Gidon, 106–112
Bujagali dam, Uganda, 158, 159–163
Bujagali Energy Limited, 159, 160, 163
Burkina Faso, 73, 74, 79
Burundi, 115

C

Cadotte, John, 150
California, 146, 149, 153–154, 155
Camps, refugee and relief services, Haiti, 128, 131–134
Canada, tidal/marine power projects, 171, 172, 173t
Cancer, 125, 126, 135, 137, 139
Carbon capture and storage, 192, 192t
Carbon emissions
    China, air and water pollution, 125–126
    desalination processes, 147
    ocean acidification effects, 34, 35, 36, 37, 39, 41–42, 59
    UK production and reduction goals, 187, 188, 189, 192
    U.S. Congress debate and policy, 38
    U.S. production, 126
Carbon Trust, 172, 173
Carbonate, 37, 41
Carrell, Severin, 34–38
Carter, Bob, 30
Catholic Relief Services (CRS), 131–134
Ceng Zhen, 80–87
Child mortality, 143

Index

Children's rights, 140, 141, 144
Chile, 88–93
    Constitution, 90, 91, 93
    elections, 92
    trading water rights has hurt citizens and environment, 88–93
China, 80–87, 121–127
    desertification, 70
    drought, 82, 83, *85*
    economic growth, 121, 123–124, 126–127
    pollution cover-ups, 121, 123, 127
    poor environmental record has poisoned water supplies, 121–127
    Three Gorges Dam, 168
    water crisis may be helped by trading water rights, 80–87
    water rationing, 122
Chinese Communist Party, 123
Ching, Lim Li, 71–79
Cholera
    Haiti, 128–134, 133*t*
    Palestine, 104
    symptoms, 129, 130
    transmission, 131, 132
Chongqing, China, 81–82, 83–86, 87
Church, John, 31, 33
Clean water needs and crises
    Bangladesh, 135, 136–139
    China, 121, 122–127
    Haiti, 128, 129–134
    India, 140, 141–144
    See also Sanitation, water
Climate change
    caused irreversible desertification in the Sahel, 63–70
    drought, 63, 64–65
    flood effects, 14–15, 20

    freshwater depletion, 88–89, 146
    hurricane effects, 15
    rainfall effects, 15
    sea level rise: Australia effects, 27–33
    sea level rise: Ireland effects, 20–26
    skeptics, and data presentation opportunities, 38
    See also Renewable energy goals of nations
Clownfish, 37
Coal power and emissions, 125–126, 180–181
Coastal cities
    Australia, water desalination, 146–147, 152, 154, 155
    Ireland coastal erosion, 24–25, 26
    U.S., water desalination, 146, 149
Coastal erosion, from global warming, 20, 21, 25
Coastal management
    Australia, 27, 28, 30, 154
    desalination effects, 154
    Ireland, 26
Coccolithophores, 41–42
Commonwealth Scientific and Industrial Research Organisation (CSIRO), 29, 30, 31
Conservation projects
    agricultural water conservation, 73, 74, 75
    coastal, 27, 28, 30
    marine protection, 35
    Middle East/Jordan River, 106, 110–111
    Nile River, 113, 115, 116
    rainwater use, 101–102, 110–111, 141, 144
    recycling, 155

Consumption statistics
  water, Israelis, 97, 98–99
  water, Palestinians, 101
Contaminated wells, 135, 136–139
Copps, Alan, 176–179
Corals
  dust harms, 65
  ocean acidification, 35, 40, 41, 42
Corporate water resources, 89–91, 93
Crowley, Mary, 43–48

D

Dams
  Brazil, hydropower and environmental harms, 164–169
  Netherlands, 16
  Nile River, 118
  Palestinian territories, 100
  security and shortfalls, 16–17
  tidal power, 182
  Uganda, hydropower, 158–163
DDT, 53, 54
de Rothschild, David, 56–57, 58–60
Dead Sea, 109–110, 111–112
Deep ocean warming, 30–31, 33
Deforestation
  desertification and, 63, 64–65, 67, 68–69
  flooding effects, 15–16
  See also Reforestation
Democratic Republic of the Congo, 115, 116, 118
Department of Energy and Climate Change (UK), 186–193
Desalination
  can help address world's clean water shortage, 105, 145–155
  energy needed, 147, 150–154

global capacity, 151*t*
history, 147–151
Desertification
  global areas, 70
  Sahel region, due to climate shifts and human action, 63–70
  Sahel region, human action reversing, 71–79
Diallo, Boubacar, 68–69
Dirección General de Aguas (DGA) (Chile), 90
Displacement, human, 165, 166–167, 169
Dolphins, 36–37
Drinking water. *See* Clean water needs and crises
Drought
  China, 82, 83, *85*
  climate change effects, 63, 64–65
  emergencies, Africa, 65–66, 72, 73
  Middle East/Jordan River, 106, 107–112
Duarte, Carlos, 42
Dust clouds, 64, 65, 66, 67
Duval, Pierre, 129, 130
Dysentery, 143

E

East Australian Current, 33
Economic growth
  China, 121, 123–124, 126–127
  India, 143
The Economist, 145–155
Ecosistemas, 92–93
Ecosystem threats/destruction
  considerations, tidal power infrastructure, 184, 186, 189
  hydroelectric dams, Brazil, 164, 166, 168

hydroelectric dams, China, 168
marine, due to acidification, 35, 37, 40, 59
marine, overfishing, 39, 42, 59
plastic in oceans, 51, 53
rivers drying, 108, 115, 116
Ecuador, 166
Egypt, 96, 113–114, 115, 116, 117–118
Elections
    Chile, 92
    India, 142, 144
Électricité de France, 183–184
Emera Inc., 171, 172
Emissions. *See* Carbon emissions
Energy companies
    China, 125
    marine/tidal power partnerships, 172–173, 174–175, 177, 179, 183–184
    water use, 89
Enersis, 174
England. *See* United Kingdom
Enríquez-Ominami, Marco, 92
Environmental court cases, 127
Environmental movement, failures, 58–59
Environmental Protection Agency, Ireland, 24t
Environmental threats/destruction
    Chinese pollution, 82, 121–127
    garbage in seas and oceans, 43–48, 49–60
    hydroelectric dams, Brazil, 164–169
    hydroelectric dams, China, 168
    hydroelectric dams, Uganda, 159–160
    Jordan River disappearing, 106, 107–112

sea level rises, 20–26, 27–33
tidal power infrastructure effects, 183–184, 186, 189, 190
water pollution (non-garbage), 82, 88–89, 107–108
water trading system, Chile, 88–93
See also Climate change
Eon, 177, 179
Eritrea, 115
Erosion, coastal, 20, 21, 25
Ethiopia, 96, 115
Europe, 170–175
    European Project on Ocean Acidification, 35–38, 40–41
    wave power's green energy, 170–175
    See also specific nations
European Project on Ocean Acidification, 35–38, 40–41
Extinctions, marine life, 35, 189

F

Famines, 66, 67, 68, 73
Firewood and desertification, 63, 64, 68–69
Fishing
    Brazil livelihoods and industry, 164, 165, 167, 168
    fishermen's cleanup of Great Pacific Garbage Patch, 43–44, 48
    overfishing, 39, 42, 59
Floods
    dams and, 16–17
    deforestation effects, 15–16
    global warming effects, 14–15, 22
    human history, 14, 16
    protection areas, 189–190
    urban areas, 24–25
Food chains, 35, 37, 40, 53
Forests, 40, 68, 76–77

France, 180–185
   energy resources, 180–181
   tidal power has been successful, 180–185
   tidal power history, 174, 180, 181–183, 184
Frente Amplio para la Nacionalizacíon del Agua (FANA), 89–90, 91
Freshwater
   polar, 22–23
   world's resources and depletion, 88–89, 90, 92, 97, 146
   See also Aquifers; Desalination; Reservoirs
Friends of the Earth Middle East, 106, 108, 110–111
Furnas Centrais Elétricas, 166, 167, 169
FusionStorm Foundation, 46

G

Garbage in seas and oceans, 43–48, 49–60
   See also Great Pacific Garbage Patch
Gaza, water crisis, 97–98, 99, 100, 101, 104
Girardi, Guido, 91
Glaciers, 22, 23, 32, 89
Global warming. *See* Climate change
Golan Heights, 96
Gomez, José Antonio, 92
Good Water Neighbors program, 110
Gore, Al, 32
Grant, Richard, 49–60
Gray, Alice, 101

Great Pacific Garbage Patch
   awareness and cleanup projects, 43–48, 56–57, 58, 59
   cleaning up will accomplish little, 49–60
   discovery, 50–51
   size, 43, 44–45, 46, *47*, 49–50, 54
Greenland ice melts, 23, 32
Greenland Ice Sheet, 23
Greenpeace, 41
Groundwater, 96, 97–98, 100, 103–104, 146
   See also Freshwater; Wells, and water access

H

Haiti, 128–134
   2010 earthquake, 128, 131
   cholera outbreak and clean water crisis, 128–134, 133*t*
Harbin, China, 121, 122–123, 126, 127
Hasbani River, 96
Health and sanitation. *See* Sanitation, water
Hebei province, China, 82
Hebron, 101–102
Hendriks, Iris, 42
Herz, Ansel, 128–134
Heyerdahl, Thor, 57
Hickey, Kieran R., 20–26
Ho, Mae-Wan, 71–79
Hosking, Rebecca, 53
Hsu, Jeremy, 14
Hunt, Julian, 14–15
Hurricane Katrina (2005), 15, 25
Hurricanes, 15, 25
Hvistendahl, Mara, 168

Hydropower
    Africa potential, 162
    global use, 162
    Uganda, 158–163
Hygiene. *See* Sanitation, water

I

Ice. *See* Ice caps; Polar ice
Ice ages, 21–22
Ice caps, 22, 23, 31, 33
Ignorance, environmental problems, 59–60
An Inconvenient Truth (documentary), 32
India, 140–144
    cities, 143
    must focus on clean water for children, 140–144
    national priorities, and election, 141–142, 144
Indian reservations, 167, 169
Indigenous peoples, 166, 167, 169
Indus River, 14
Industrial accidents, 122–125, 127
Infant mortality, 66, 68
International Desalination Association, 146, 152
International Finance Corporation (IFC), 160
International Panel on Climate Change (IPCC) data, 24t, 29, 33
International Rivers, 166
Ireland, 20–26
    coastal urban areas, 24–25, 26
    ice caps and sheets, 22
    will be hurt by sea level rise due to global warming, 20–26
IRIN News, 135–139

Irrigation
    African agriculture, 78, 117, 118
    groundwater pollution, 98
    Middle Eastern agriculture, 100, 102, 103, 108
    Nile River, 117, 118
Israel, 94–105
    conflicts history, 94–95, 96, 97, 106
    creation/early history, 94, 109
    occupation, 99–101, 105
    water crisis, and drought/ Jordan River, 107, 108, 109, 110, 111
    water crisis, and theft of Palestinian water, 94–105
Israeli Civil Administration, 97
Israeli military, 97, 98, 101–102, 104
Israeli-Palestinian peace agreements, 97, 105
Ives, James, 172

J

Jayyousi, Anan, 99
Jialing River, 83
Jilin Petrochemical Company, 127
Jordan, 95–96, 100, 106, 107, 108, 109, 110, 111
Jordan River, 95, 96, 106, 107–112

K

Kaisei (ship), 45, 46
Kennedy, John F., 146
Kenya, 73, 75–76, 115, 116
Kielburger, Craig, 140–144
Kielburger, Marc, 140–144
Kininmonth, William, 30–31, 32, 33

Knutson, Thomas R., 15
Kyalimpa, Joshua, 113–118

L

Laffoley, D.d'A, 36
Lake Tiberias, 95, 109
Lake Victoria, 113, 114–116, 161
Land rights vs. water rights, 90
Landslides, 168
Larwanou, Mahamane, 77–78
Leal, Susan, 117
Lebanon, 96
Levees, Netherlands, 16
Litani River, 96
Litter, on-land, 47, 51, 52–53
Little Ice Age, 22
Locusts, 65–66
Loeb, Sidney, 149
Lorenz, Andreas, 121–127

M

Madden, James, 27–33
Madeira River, 164, 165–169
Malaria, 167
Mali, 64, 65, 66, 68, 79
Mao Zedong, 125, 126
Marine life
    aquaculture, 81
    desalination processes, effects, 153–154
    desertification and dust effects, 65
    extinctions, 35, 189
    harms from plastics, 53–54, 55
    threats of ocean acidification, 35–37, 59
    tidal power infrastructure effects, 183–184, 186, 189, 190
Marine power. *See* Tidal power; Wave power

Markets, water, 80–87, 88–93
Media consumption, 59
Membranes, water, 149, 150, 151, 152–153
Meningitis, 104
Mercury, 54
Middle East, 106–112
    Israel's theft of Palestinian water, 94–105
    water crisis a result of failures of regional governments, 106–112
    water desalination, 146, 148, 149, 150–151
Midlandian Ice Age, 22
Mills, 181–182, 184–185
Minc, Carlos, 169
Mining, 89
Mitterrand, Danielle, 91
Moore, Charles, 50–51, 52, 56, 57
Movimiento Amplio Social (MAS) (Chile), 92
Muhit, Abul Maal Abdul, 136
Multi-stage flash (desalination), 148–149
Mumbo, Gordon, 118
Muramuzi, Frank, 115
Museveni, Yoweri, 159–160

N

Namuyangu, Jennifer, 117
NASA photography, 65
National Oceanic and Atmospheric Administration (NOAA), 45
National Tidal Centre (Australia), 28, 30, 31
Nationalization, water supplies, 88, 91–93
Natural disasters. *See* Drought; Floods; Hurricanes

Index

Natural gas, 181
Navarro, Alejandro, 92
Navies, garbage dumping, 51
Ndombe, Henrietta, 118
Netherlands, 16
New Delhi, India, 143
New Horizon (ship), 45
New South Wales, Australia, 27, 28–31, 33
Niger, 65–66, 73, 75, 76–79
Nigeria, 73, 74
Niiler, Pearn, 54
Nile Basin Commission, 116
Nile Basin Discourse Forum, 114
Nile Basin Initiative, 114–115, 117–118
Nile River, 113–118
    beneficial flooding, 14
    dams, 158, 159–160, 161
    history, 117
    size, and populations served, 96, 114, 117
    water rights struggles, 96, 113–118
Nile River Basin Cooperative Framework, 115
Nitrogen dioxide emissions, 125–126
North Atlantic ocean, acidification, 38
North Pacific ocean
    acidification, 38
    Subtropical Gyre, 50
North Pacific Trash Gyre
    awareness and cleanup projects, 43–48, 56–57, 58, 59
    cleaning up will accomplish little, 49–60
    discovery, 50–51
    size, 43, 44–45, 46, 47, 49–50, 54

Nuclear power, 179, 181, 183, 189, 192, 192t
Nurdles, 52, 56

O

Occupational safety and health, China, 123–124
Ocean acidification
    past and future, 36
    reports, 35–38, 40–41
    seriousness overstated, 39–42
    threats and dangers, 34–38, 59
Ocean Conservancy, 44, *47*
Ocean garbage. *See* Great Pacific Garbage Patch
Ocean power. *See* Tidal power; Wave power
Ocean Voyages Institute, 46
Ocean water level changes. *See* Sea level changes
Ocean water thermal expansion and effects, 22–23, 30–31, 33
Oceans United, 40
Odebrecht, 166
OpenHydro, 172
Orrego, Juan Pablo, 92–93
Oslo Accords (1993), 97, 105
Osmosis, 149
Oster, Shai, *85*
Overfishing
    more serious problem than acidification, 39, 42
    most urgent ocean problem, 59
Overpopulation, Sahel region, 63, 64, 68–69

P

Pacific ocean
    cleaning up garbage patch will accomplish little, 49–60

great garbage patch should be cleaned up, 43–48
Pakistan floods, 2010, 14–15
Palakudiyil, Tom, 142, 143–144
Palestine, 94–105
    water crisis: drought and Jordan River, 107, 108, 110, 111
    water crisis: Israel's water theft, 94–105
Palestine Economic Policy Research Institute, 99
Palestinian-Israeli peace agreements, 97, 105
Palestinian Water Authority, 97–98, 103
Paper production, 87
Partido Radical (PR) (Chile), 92
Partido Socialista (PS) (Chile), 92
Partlow, Joshua, 164–169
Partners in Health, 134
PCBs, 53, 54
Pelamis Wave Power, 174, 176–179
Peng Guangcan, 80–87
PET plastic, 58
pH levels, 41, 42, 59
    See also Acidification of oceans
Phillips, Helen, 35
Photodegredation, 52
Pierre, Jacques, 132
Pinochet, Augusto, 89, 90, 91
Plankton
    ocean acidification, 35, 40, 41–42
    outweighed by plastic in oceans, 49, 51, 54–55
    plastic content, 53, 54
Plastic bags, 50, 53, 58
Plastics
    cleaning up oceans will accomplish little, 49–60

    disposable vs. reuse-able, 49, 57–58
    invention, 54
    ocean cleanup projects, 43–48, 56–57
    physical properties, 52
    recycling, 43, 47, 56, 57
    reducing use, 49, 57–58
    ubiquitous nature, 55
Plastiki (boat), 57, 58, 59
Polar ice
    freshwater stores, 22
    melting, sea level effects, 20, 22–23, 26, 31, 32, 33
Polgreen, Lydia, 76–77
Pollution. *See* Air pollution; Water pollution
Pollution trading, 86
Population increases
    Africa, 64, 65, 68, 74, 76
    India, 143
    Middle East, 97–98
    worldwide, 146
Porto, Marcio, 166, 167
Portugal, 176–179
Privatized water. *See* Water rights
Project Kaisei, 43–48
Purification tablets, 144

Q

Queensland, Australia, 30
Quillagua, Chile, 89

R

Rainfall
    Chinese droughts, 83
    climate change effects, 15, 21, 64
    harvesting programs, 110–111, 141, 144
    Nile River levels and, 115

Index

Palestinian rainwater collection, 101–102
Sahel region, 65–66, 72–73
Rajoub, Abdel-Rahman, 102
Ramahi, Sawsan, 94–105
Rance River, 174, 180, 182–183, 183–184
Rationing of water, 122
Recycling
    end products, 56, 57, 58
    plastics, rescued from ocean, 43, 47
    rates and laws, 47, 49
    wastewater, 155, 161
Red-Dead Project, 109–110, 111–112
Red Sea, 109, 111–112
Rees, Nathan, 28
Reforestation, 16
    China, 70
    Niger, 76–77, 78–79
    Sahel region, 71
Refugees
    Mali, 65
    Palestine, 105
Reij, Chris, 79
Relief organizations, Haiti, 128, 131–134
Religious significance of Jordan River, 107, 111
Renewable energy goals of nations, 125, 179, 181, 187, 189
Renewable energy resources. *See* Solar power; Tidal power; Wind power
Reservoirs
    Brazilian dam-created, 166–167
    Israel/Palestine, 96, 97, 100, 103
    reclaimed water storage, 155
    tidal power, 182
    world resources, 146
Reverse osmosis, 149–150, 154, 155
Ridley, Matt, 39–42
Rights trading, water. *See* Water rights
Rillieux, Norbert, 148
Rio Grande, 108
River management, 108, 109–110, 111–112
Rogers, Peter, 117
Rubaihayo, Patrick, 116–117
Rudd, Kevin, 28
Ruiz-Tagle, Eduardo Frei, 92
Runoff, 42
Russia, 123
Rwanda, 115, 117
RWE, 171

S

Sahel, 63–70, 71–79
    climate shifts and human action have caused irreversible desertification, 63–70
    crop areas, 67*t*, 78
    human action reversing desertification, 71–79
Sahel Institute, 68
Salamanders, 81
Saltwater desalination. *See* Desalination
Sandstorms, 64, 65, 66
Sanitation, water
    Bangladesh, 136
    Haiti, 128, 130, 131–134
    India, 140, 141–144
    Palestine, and Israel water theft, 98, 104
Scott, Mark, 170–175

Scripps Institution of Oceanography, 45, 54
Sea creatures. *See* Marine life; Seabirds
Sea level changes
   global warming, Australia, 27–33
   global warming, Ireland, 20–26
   historical rates and averages, 22, 24t, 27, 29, 31
   historical shifts and patterns, 21–22
   twenty-first century rates and predictions, 23, 24t, 26, 28–29, 32, 33
Sea of Galilee, 95, 109
Seabirds
   estuary habitats, 186, 189, 190
   harms from plastics, 53, 55
Seawater desalination. *See* Desalination
Senegal, 73, 79
Sengupta, Somini, 143
Separation wall, Israel/Palestine, 102–104, 108
Settlements, Israeli, in Palestinian territories, 100, 101
Severe Acute Respiratory Syndrome (SARS), 127
Severn Estuary Project (UK), 184, 186–193
Shalita, Steven, 158–163
Shellfish, 37, 40, 41, 42
Shipping garbage, 51
Shortages of water
   Chile, and water rights trading, 89–90, 91
   China, and accidents/pollution, 122, 123, 127
   China, and water rights trading, 80–87
   desalination as solution, 145–155
   India, 141, 143
   Palestinian territories, Israeli water theft, 94–105
   Western Australia, 155
   See also Drought
Shoumatoff, Alex, 63–70
Silting, rivers, 183–184
Singapore, 155
Smell sense, fishes, 37
Socialist Party, Chile, 92
Solar power, 171, 175
Songhua River (China), 121, 122–123, 125, 127
Sounds, underwater, 36–37
Sourirajan, Srinivasa, 149
Sovereignty, Palestinian, 105
Spain, marine energy, 173, 175
Starfish, 37, 42
Stewart, Robert, 67t
Sudan, 96, 113–114, 115, 116, 117
Sugar refining, 147–148
Sulfur emissions, 125–126
Sutter, Peter, 46
Switkes, Glenn, 166, 167
Syria, 95–96, 106, 107, 108, 109, 111

T

Tamimi, Abdel Rahman, 97
Tanzania, 115, 116
Thermal desalination, 148–150, 154
Three Gorges Dam (China), 168
Tidal power
   cost comparisons, 188, 189, 192t
   European green energy source, 170–175
   France, success, 180–185

Index

history, 181–182
not feasible in Britain's Severn estuary, 186–193
See also Wave power
Tindimugaya, Callist, 116
Tinning, Matt, 44
Tongliang, China, 81–82, 83–86, 86, 87
Toxic pollutants, 122–125, 127
See also Water pollution
Trash in seas and oceans, 43–48, 49–60
See also Great Pacific Garbage Patch
Turtles, 53
Typhoid/typhoid fever, 104, 143

U

Uganda, 158–163
hydropower dams provide needed electricity, 158–163
Nile River water rights, 113, 115, 116, 117
Uncontacted tribes, Brazil, 167
Underwater sound, 36–37
United Kingdom, 186–193
calls for water power projects, 184–185
tidal/marine power projects, 171, 172, 173, 173t, 174–175, 176–179
tidal power not feasible in Severn estuary, 184, 186–193
United Nations
Copenhagen climate conference, 2009, 34, 35
desertification conferences, 73
Haitian cholera outbreak, 129–130
Human Development Report, 66
Israel/Palestine negotiations, 105
Office for the Coordination of Humanitarian Affairs, 135
requests for projects, 40
United Nations Environment Programme
budget, 59
land surface data, 67t, 69–70
plastics harms data, 51, 53
United States Agency for International Development (USAID), 132–133

V

Van Slambrouck, Paul, 43–48
Varel, John, 46–47
Venture capitalist investment, marine power, 172, 175, 177–178, 188
Vervoort, Willem, 16–17
Virilio, Paul, 54

W

Walsh, Christopher M., 158–163
Warne-Smith, Drew, 27–33
Wasted water, 99
Wastewater, 87, 154, 155
Water Code, Chile, 90
Water consumption rates, 97, 98–99, 101
Water pollution
accidents, 122–125, 127
Chile, 88–89
China, 82, 121–127
desalination wastes, 154
Jordan River, 107–108
ocean garbage, 43–48, 49–60
Water rights
defining, 84
Nile River struggles, 113–118
trading, alleviating China's water crisis, 80–87

217

trading system has hurt citizens and environment in Chile, 88–93
Wave power
  history, 181–182
  may become important source of green energy in Europe, 170–175
  projects have failed in Portugal, 176–179
  See also Tidal power
Wavegen, 173
Wazzani River, 96
Wells, and water access
  Bangladesh, 135–139
  China, 122, 123
  India, 141
  Israeli-controlled, 96, 97, 98, 100, 101, 103, 104
  Niger, 78
Wen Jiabao, 126
Wesoff, Eric, 173
West Bank, 96, 97–98, 99, 100, 101–104
Whales, 36–37, 54
Williams, Robert, 180–185
Wind power, 171, 173, 175, 186, 189, 192, 192t

Witte, Benjamin, 88–93
World Bank, 90, 109, 110
World Bank Group, 159, 161
World Health Organization (WHO)
  arsenic in drinking water, 137, 138
  water consumption recommendations, 98
Wyatt, Stephen, 173

X

Xingu River, 168

Y

Yangtze River, 124–125, 168
Yarmouk River and river basin, 95–96, 109, 111
Yellow River, 108
Yiwu, China, 82

Z

Zhou Jigang, 80–87
Zhou Ying, 86

www.ingramcontent.com/pod-product-compliance
Lightning Source LLC
Chambersburg PA
CBHW071911290426
44110CB00013B/1355